THE INFLUENCE OF ENGLISH LITERATURE ON URDU LITERATURE

BY

SAYYID 'ABDU'L-LAṬĪF

LONDON

FORSTER GROOM & CO., LIMITED

15 CHARING CROSS, S.W. 1

1924

CONTENTS

PART III

RESULTS OF ENGLISH INFLUENCE

CHAPTER IV

CHAPTER V

CHAPTER VI

CHAPTER VII

TRANSLITERATION

The following system which varies very slightly from Blumhardt's has been followed in the work. Articles and vowel-points correspond to pronunciation :—

ب	b	ص	ṣ
پ	p	ض	ẓ
ت	t	ط	t̤
ٹ	ṭ	ظ	z̤
ث	s̤	ع	ʻ
ج	j	غ	g͟h
چ	ch	ف	f
ح	ḥ	ق	q
خ	k͟h	ك	k
د	d	گ	g
ڈ	d̲	ل	l
ذ	ẕ	م	m
ر	r	ن	n
ڑ	ṛ	و	w, etc.
ز	z	ه	h
ژ	zh	ء	ʼ
س	s	ى	y, etc.
ش	sh		

INTRODUCTION

During the last century and a half of the British connection there have been at work in India several forces, political, religious, economic, social and literary, which have brought about a profound change over the thought and life of its people. It is a change which may be described as the result of the interaction of two distinctly different cultures and civilisations, one so typically Eastern as the Indian, and the other so fully representative of the Western as the English. To estimate the character and extent of such a change in all its manifestations, however fruitful and desirable, is neither possible within a short compass such as the writer has set to himself here, nor is it a work for any single individual. It is a task which will occupy the lifetime, not of one, but several collaborators, each interested in a separate phase of this interesting problem.

In the following pages, however, an attempt will be made to deal with the subject in one of its important bearings, viz. literature, as signifying in a definite and readily ascertainable form the wider working of this problem. The department of literature has been singled out for examination, for the simple and obvious reason that it is in this, more than in any other, that the national life and genius of a people is generally expressed in a comprehensive manner. It should not, however, be supposed that the entire output of modern Indian literature would necessarily be brought under review. For not only would that be a stupendous effort involving the study of all that has appeared in the form of literature in at least a dozen of the more important languages of India, but a task ordinarily beyond the power of any single investigator. Besides, such an undertaking, even were it possible, is not worth the labour, as the study would amount to nothing more than noting the same tendencies and features, over and over again, possibly in varying proportion, in one language after another, supported as it would be necessary, by parallel illustrations from each. To avoid, therefore, needless elaboration and probable repetition, as well as to promote the interests of clearness and brevity, the writer proposes to confine his attention to the literature of one language such as, in his opinion, is best suited to illustrate the object in view.

For this purpose he has chosen Urdu literature as the subject of his investigation. There are several reasons which have prompted his choice. Of these one is that Urdu is the most widely prevalent language of India, indeed the only common speech, and as such entitled to primary consideration. Another is the fact that owing to the peculiar conditions under which it rose and its marvellous capacity for assimilation of new words and ideas, it has been affected more than any other language by the impact of Western thought and by the literary ideals which have flowed into it through the language and literature of England.

The present is therefore an inquiry into the several influences from English literature which have contributed to the growth and development of Urdu literature. It is hoped that the study may prove, in however small a measure, helpful to students of comparative literature interested in discovering and appraising the results of the interaction of cultures differing in essentials one from the other.

Three different methods of approach to the subject

suggest themselves. One would be to take one department of literature after another and notice the various new influences discernible in each. This method, while apparently systematic, is apt to result in much overlapping and obscure the main results of investigation. Another would be to make a linear or chronological division of the whole period under review, in so far as it is susceptible of any division into well-marked epochs, with distinct characteristics and tendencies of their own. The subject, however, does not lend itself to such treatment, as English influence has been in effective operation only during the last sixty years or so, and its different streams have been simultaneous rather than successive. A third would be to unravel the main threads of this foreign influence and to pursue the working of each idea through the different branches of Urdu literature. Of these methods the last has been preferred, because it is both logical and scientific and at the same time helps to present the subject in a clearer and more intelligible form. It also enables us to take a wider sweep of the whole range of modern literature, both English and Urdu, and to get behind its form and content to the underlying forces, political, social, religious and literary, of which literature is but the expression.

As language and literature are organic growths, and a particular phase of their history cannot be fully studied without a reference to their past and the forces that have shaped them, it has been found necessary to make a rapid survey of the early history of Urdu before the commencement of English influence. Accordingly, the first part of the study will be confined to this as a preliminary background to the subject.

In the second part an attempt will be made to explain the several channels and agencies through which English influence has made itself felt and the different points at which it has impinged upon the life and thought of the country.

This would naturally lead us on to the third and the most important part of our study, which will analyse and sift the main ideas which have been at work and pursue them right across the several branches of literature.

The difficulties met with in the prosecution of this task have been many. In the first place, no attempt of a similar nature, in however limited a manner, has been made by any writer hitherto. The studies of British scholars have been practically confined to the structure and vocabulary of the Urdu language, and do not extend to the form and substance of its literature. Secondly, the biographies, most of them meagre and fragmentary, of famous literary men rarely throw any light on the influences which had gone to shape their thought and expression. They are mainly chronicles of the leading events of their life and but seldom reveal the working of their inner mind. The writer has therefore had to fall back upon the literature itself, voluminous and varied as it is, as the main source of his study. An exhaustive survey even of this is not possible in a short time, and also in view of the incomplete equipment of the libraries in London. The newspaper literature which perhaps might show the process in its gradual growth has not, to the knowledge of the writer, been preserved completely in any library either in England or India, nor even all the works of the minor writers which might have offered some suggestive clues. He has therefore had to content himself with the works chiefly of the leading writers of the period under review and of such others as he has been able to obtain either here or from India.

His difficulties, such as they are, have been greatly lightened not only by the encouragement and facilities so generously afforded to him by Prof. Sir Israel Gollancz, under whom he has had the honour of pursuing his studies and to whom, in fact, he owes the very idea of the subject, but also by the valuable guidance very kindly given him from time to time by Prof. Sir Thomas Arnold, especially in the treatment of the writings of the leaders of the Aligarh educational movement with which Prof. Arnold was himself personally associated for some time. He has also to acknowledge his indebtedness to Dr. A. W. Reed, King's College, for the kind and helpful suggestions he has received from him in the presentation of the Thesis, and to Dr. Col. D. C. Phillott for having very generously read the final proofs during his absence from England and systematised the transliteration of oriental terms while the work was in the press.

S. A.-Laṭīf.

PART I

URDU LITERATURE BEFORE ENGLISH INFLUENCE

CHAPTER I

HISTORICAL SURVEY OF EARLY URDU LITERATURE

(i) IMPORTANCE OF THE URDU LANGUAGE

THE Urdu language occupies a peculiarly important place in the life of the people of India. While languages spoken in North India and Deccan, such as Assamese, Bengali, Punjabi, Oriya, and Mahrati—languages which claim Indo-Aryan descent—or those prevailing in the south, such as Telugu, Canarese, or Malayalam, owning Dravidian origin, are little known outside of the limited areas to which they have severally lent their name, Urdu is not merely spoken in the land of its birth, Delhi and the surrounding country, but is widely known and understood all over India. In one or other of its dialectal variations this language is the mother-tongue of over a hundred millions, or nearly a third of the population of the country.[1] In addition to this, another hundred millions use it as an indispensable second language in their daily intercourse, not only in the bazaar or market-place, as the term "Urdu" implies, but even in polite society.[2] Indeed during recent years its influence has extended far beyond the confines of India. Afghanistan, Baluchistan, Southern Persia, Mesopotamia, Hejaz, the

[1] Nearly two-thirds of the Indian Muslims, numbering over eighty millions, and most of the Hindu urban population in the United Provinces and parts of the Eastern Punjab and the Nizam's Dominions speak it in their homes.

[2] Among those who can easily understand Urdu may be included all the people whose mother-tongue is one or other of the following dialects allied to Urdu, and which are grouped together by Sir

east coast of Africa, Burma, and the Malay Archipelago are some of the outlying countries where it is slowly making headway. It has thus not only won a more or less recognised position as the common language of India, but promises by virtue of its intrinsic qualities to play one day the rôle of the *lingua franca* of the East.

Although this extension of influence is a comparatively modern phenomenon, and the term "Urdu" [1] itself is also of modern application, it should not be forgotten that Urdu as a language represents but a phase—the latest of course—of a development of a very ancient language. Its immediate ancestor is the *Brajbhāsha*, which in turn can be traced back to the primary Prakrit prevalent in the Vedic period among the Aryan races who had settled down in the Madhya Desha, the Midland, or the country round about Delhi and Agra. An account of the rise and development of this Prakrit into Sanskrit and ultimately into some of the modern North Indian vernaculars, including Urdu, however interesting, does not come within the scope of our subject.[2] But the fact should be borne in mind that modern Urdu bears on it the impress both of the languages and the

---

Charles Lyall under the common name of "Hindustani" or the speech of Hindustan :—

"*Marwari* and *Jaipuri* (Rajputana).
Brajbhasha (Mathura and Agra).
Kanauji (Lower Ganges-Jumna Doab and Western Rohilkhand).
Eastern Hindi or *Awadhi* and *Baiswari* (Eastern Rohilkhand, Oudh, and the Benares Division of the United Provinces).
Bihari (Behar or Mithila, comprising several distinct dialects)."
(*Encycl. Brit.*, 11th ed., Vol. XIII., Hindustani Language.)

[1] Originally the name of the military headquarters of the Mongols at Qaraqoram. The term eventually came to be applied in India to the language that took its rise in the Camp of the Moghul Emperors.

[2] For an account of this process, see Grierson; *Imperial Gazetteer of India*, New Series, Vol. I. ch. vii. See also *J.R.A.S.* for 1904, pp. 435 and 457.

thoughts of all those races, either Indian or foreign, who in the long and chequered history of India have held the mastery of Delhi or have come into contact with the life of its people. One may liken it to a huge and expansive stream into which have flowed at different stages of its progress diverse tributaries, some large, some small, some even disturbing cataracts and mountain rivulets, all bringing with them the colour of the beds through which they have passed and giving together to the principal stream a tint or hue which is altogether fascinating.

(ii) Early Literature—Hindu Contribution

With a long and interesting history such as this language has had, one will naturally expect to find in it a literature hoary as its age and rich as the proverbial riches of India. But, strange as it may seem, facts belie the expectation. Owing to a peculiar combination of circumstances, the original language of Delhi never could emerge till about A.D. 1100 from the position to which Sanskrit had relegated it from the very beginning, viz. of a "Prakrit" or the "natural, rustic, unartificial" tongue of the common people. Sanskrit, "polished or purified," as it means, remained all along the language of literary expression. The rise of Buddhism in the fifth century B.C., with its attempt to impart its message through the Prakrit, no doubt gave the vernacular for a while an importance such as it had never enjoyed before. And although during the succeeding centuries it received, at different times, a certain amount of attention from men of letters, it was not until the establishment of the Muslim power in India that the vernacular speech had the chance and the necessary encouragement to assume a distinctly literary character.[1]

[1] The term "Prakrit" is retained throughout to denote the vernacular speech for the sake of clearness, although it was known by different names at different stages of its progress. See Grierson, *Imperial Gazetteer of India*, Vol. I. ch. vii.

The Muslims who, from the eleventh century onwards, began to pour into India from the North-west, first under the "Afghans" and then under the "Moguls," came of different races: nevertheless, they had together a distinctive character of their own which marked them out as a class of people differing from those of the soil, not merely in physical appearance, strength or endurance, but also in their language, religion, culture, and in their general outlook on life. These invaders, unlike the Greeks under Alexander or the British in our own time, chose to settle down in India and make it their home. The contact and intercourse which, in consequence, followed between the two peoples, whether in times of war or of peace, covering a period of over 800 years, have naturally and inevitably produced far-reaching effects on the language and literature of the country.

The new-comers brought with them a highly developed language of their own, viz. Persian, which, in spite of the fact that some of them were originally born to one or other of the Turanian dialects of Central Asia, they all claimed as their common speech. This Persian which they employed was not the Persian spoken in the time of the Sāsānians (A.D. 229–652) or in earlier periods, but the Persian which, as the result of Arab conquest of Persia and its acceptance of the religion of the Arabs, had grown into a form of speech which clearly bore on it the hall-mark of Islam.[1] The Muslim invaders were proud of this language and disdained to invoke the help of Sanskrit for literary or administrative purposes. So great was the vogue given by them to Persian, that not only during the days of their long domination of nearly 500 years, but even under British rule down to 1832, it remained the language of the Court and of the Administration.

[1] See Browne, *A Literary History of Persia*, Vol. II. pp. 4–6. Also Muḥammad Ḥusayn Āzād, *Sakhundān-i-Fars*, Third Lecture, Lahore, 1898.

Under such conditions, what an enormous influence must Persian have exercised on the language and literature of the country! The Muslim emperors, especially the Moguls, were great patrons of learning. With all their loyalty and adherence to their national language, they never forgot the interests of the indigenous literatures, particularly of *Brajbhāsha*, the vernacular of Delhi. In fact, it was part of their official policy to encourage and foster it by holding out liberal rewards to men of talent whose writings in the vernacular speech deserved recognition, and by conferring upon them the title of *Kabī Rāj*, or Poet Laureate. The example of the emperors was followed by the Governors and prominent noblemen, both Hindu and Muslim, who took pride in keeping with them laureates of their own who would sing their praise and beguile their idle hours. Prominent among those who flourished at the Mogul Court may be mentioned Raja Bīrbal, Tān Sen, Gangā Prasād, Sundar, and the Tripathi Brothers. These Hindu poets, out of regard for their patrons, whom they were intent on pleasing, tried to make their productions more and more intelligible to the latter by the incorporation into their writings of words and phrases and literary ideas borrowed from Persian and through Persian from Arabic. Partly because of this conscious effort, and partly because of the atmospheric influence due to an increasing intercourse between the rulers and the ruled, not only was the *Brajbhāsha* gradually Persianised, but the literature in it and in the allied dialects which was produced during the early Muslim rule, whether under Court influence or independent of it, was greatly affected by the impact of Muslim thought and Muslim culture.

This literature, which is the precursor of Urdu literature, may be classified into three groups. The first consists of bardic chronicles like those of Chānd Bardoi and Jayānāik (twelfth century) and Sārang Dhar (fourteenth century), written under the stress of a national struggle with the invader. The second consists of devotional hymns and religious songs, such as those of Kabīr (1440–1518), the founder of the sect of Kabīrpanth, Gurū Nānak (1469–1538), the originator of Sikhism, and Tulsī Dās (1532–1623), the author of the great religious epic of *Rāmāyan*, all intended to supply the growing popular need for spiritual knowledge and guidance which was not easily accessible through Sanskrit and which was in a measure denied under the old Brahminic ideals. The last group is composed of erotic poetry.

This literature, it should be noticed, is almost entirely in verse. It is written in the indigenous script, the Nāgari, and follows indigenous rules of prosody and composition. Although some of the writers, such as Kabīr, of whom mention is already made, and Malik Muḥammad Jayāsī, author of the famous romance *Padmāwatī*, were Muslims, and although this literature, which now goes under the name of Hindi, bears clear traces of Muslim influence, it is, nevertheless, in form, in substance and in purpose, essentially a Hindu contribution. A large majority of the Muslim settlers neither thought very much of it nor took any part in its cultivation. The best period of this literature lasted from the middle of the twelfth to the close of the sixteenth century.[1]

(iii) Early Literature—Muslim Contribution

By this time, owing to the forces described above, *Brajbhāsha* had been gradually so permeated with words and expressions of Persian origin that the Muslims had no difficulty in getting naturalised to it. In fact by the beginning of the seventeenth century, when Shāh Jahān came to power, a very large section of the Muslims, whether descendants of the early invaders or new converts to their faith,

[1] See F. E. Keay, *Hindi Literature*, Calcutta, 1916.

living either in the metropolis and the surrounding country or in the distant colonies of the south where it had been carried by Muslim armies during the earlier reigns, had come to employ in their homes, and in their daily intercourse outside, only this new form of *Brajbhāsha*, which by now had assumed a new name, *Urdu* or the language of the camp or of its mixed population.[1] Persian had, of course, still its sway: it was still the language of the Court and of the Administration and the only language in which it was considered proper to undertake any serious literature and even ordinary correspondence. But as a spoken tongue on any large scale, among Muslims, its days were past. Urdu had usurped its place.

When this stage in its progress was reached, the literary class among Muslims naturally felt a fancy to adopt it for literary purposes. There was, however, a strong prejudice among the orthodox against such a course. To them Urdu was still a hybrid and rustic jargon unworthy of literary cultivation. This prejudice was strongest in the metropolis, where there was always a large conservative element worshipping antiquated ideals. The response to this new craving in literature, therefore, came not from Delhi, where the Urdu language had its birth, but from the Deccan, where, under the local dialectical appellation of *Dakhanī*, it had found a stronghold in the independent Muslim Courts of South India, where Persian had long ceased to be a spoken language.[2] Prominent among those who were associated with this movement is the name of Shams Walīu'llāh (1680–1720) of Aurangabad, who during the reign of the Mogul Emperor, Muḥammad Shāh, migrated to Delhi and paved the way for the rise of those successive generations of literary men who, during an amazingly short period, have

[1] See Mīr Amman's preface to *Bāgh o Bahār*.

[2] See Sir Charles Lyall in *Encycl. Brit.*, 11th ed., Vol. XIII; Hindustani Literature.

succeeded in raising the rugged speech of Delhi to the status of a first-rate literary language.[1]

The honour and credit of this achievement is shared between Delhi and Lucknow, the two great centres of Muslim culture and learning. But Delhi seems to deserve it more than Lucknow, for it was in Delhi that the pioneers of this early Urdu literature were born or flourished, men like Mīr Dard, Rafī'u 's-Sawdā, Mīr Taqī, Qalandar Bakhsh Jur'at, Mīr Ḥasan, Shāh Naṣīr, M'umin Khān, Shaykh Ibrāhīm Zawq and Asadu'llāh Khān Ghālib, who, whatever their limitations and weaknesses, have rendered distinct service to the cause of literature by purifying, polishing, enriching and preparing the language to serve in the hands of those who came after them, during the present days of English influence, as a satisfactory and healthy medium of literary expression.

The characteristics of their literature, so far as relevant to the subject of our inquiry, will be discussed in the following chapter. But mention should be made here of the fact that the main stimulus to the growth of this literature was supplied by Muslim writers who were not particularly conversant with indigenous script and indigenous literature. They knew but one script and knew but one literature, viz. the Islamic Persian. So when the inclination was felt to attempt literary composition in the new language, they naturally adopted the Persian script and followed the Persian literary ideals. The step had its own points of strength and weakness. The strength lay in the fact that the writers had ready to hand, for use, approved models and a full-fledged system of prosody and literary technique, and its weakness in the blind faith with which they regarded this system as immutable and all sufficient and in the timidity and lack of vision to strike a new line of their own.

[1] See *Āb-i-Ḥayāt*, Lahore, 1883.

What followed was, that until the advent of English influence, all that went under the name of Urdu literature, which is entirely in verse, was all imitative, artificial and uninspiring. This was as it should have been. For if literature is the reflex of national life, it should not be surprising that Urdu literature of the first 150 years, beginning approximately with the decline of the great Mogul Empire and ending with its final tragic disappearance in 1857, was a literature groaning, like the degenerate Muslim society of the times, under its own dead weight and yet not knowing that it was groaning. Hedged in by hard-and-fast rules, revelling in a narrow circle of thin and hackneyed ideas, and making a virtue of extravagance, meaningless subtleties, far-fetched conceits and empty declamation, this early literature dragged on a dreary existence till at one time, after the great Indian Mutiny, when the fortunes of Islam in India were at their lowest ebb, it almost seemed that the shadow of death was fast closing around it.[1]

Fortunately, however, this did not come to pass. For with the final establishment of the British power in India and the restoration of peace and order, there began to flow into the country diverse influences of Western culture and Western literary ideals which speedily infused fresh life into the withering plant of Urdu literature, and stimulated its growth with surprising rapidity.

[1] See also Introduction to *Āb-i-Ḥayāt*, Lahore, 1883.

CHAPTER II

CHARACTERISTICS OF THE EARLY URDU LITERATURE

BEFORE we examine the influences from the West, it is necessary to discuss at some length the ideals which were responsible for the growth of the early form of Urdu literature and its leading characteristics, in order that we may be able, by comparison, to estimate properly the value and importance of the new literature. Certain questions suggest themselves in this connection: What does this early literature consist of? What are its forms? What its substance? Does it stand for any ideal or ideals? or has it any message to convey? What are the elements of its strength and of its weakness and how did it come to possess the one or the other? In short, what are the scope and the quality of this literature, and what are the forces that created it?

(i) CONDITION OF THE MUSLIM COMMUNITY DURING THIS PERIOD

We shall take the last question first: What were those forces and ideals which shaped this early literature? An answer to this must be sought in the circumstances of the life of those among whom it grew and developed. For this we shall have to look into the political, social, and religious condition of the Indian Muslims during the 150 years from the death of Awrangzayb in 1707 to the final extinction of the Mogul Empire in 1858.

Political.[1]—The reign of Awrangzayb (1658–1707) had

[1] Among *English* works dealing with the political history of Indian Muslims from 1707 to 1857, see especially: (1) Lane-Poole, *Medieval India*; (2) Sydney Owen, *Fall of the Mogul Empire*; (3) H. G. Keene, *Hindustan under the Free-Lances*; (4) A. Lyall, *Rise and Expansion of British Dominions in India*; (5) Hunter, *Indian Musulmans*; (6) Sir Sayyid Aḥmad, *Causes of the Indian Mutiny*.

witnessed the high-water mark of the Muslim power in India. Never before had their empire in India been so extensive as under the rule of this great Puritan. Still, strange as it may appear, it was during this very reign that the decline of their power began. Indeed the seeds of decay had already been sown. The Muslims were no longer the same hardy and robust warriors as the veterans of Babur who had swept over the country and laid the foundation of his empire. The enervating climate of the country, and the luxurious ease and indolence of the Courts of Jahāngīr and Shāh Jahān had bred effeminacy, and sapped and undermined those qualities and virtues which at one time had made their ancestors so powerful. The Muslim nobles, who now followed the camp of Awrangzayb, or carried on the administration in the different parts of his empire, were mere "grandees in petticoats," "who went to war in palanquins." These were not, evidently, the type of men who could run and preserve big empires. Few of them really bore any particular love for the imperial throne. Indeed, some of them would have been only too glad to strike a blow at it had opportunity presented itself. It was only the indomitable will and the indefatigable energy and power of organisation of the emperor, and the fear and terror inspired by the austerity of his personal life, which kept in check, not only the disloyal noblemen within his camp, but those turbulent elements outside, the Sikhs in the Punjab and the Mahrattas in the Deccan, who were to burst forth and shake the empire to its foundations, as soon as the iron hand of the emperor was laid in dust.

Bahādur Shāh I (1707–1712), the aged son of Awrangzayb, who succeeded him, though he might probably have, under better conditions, played a part worthy of a scion of the House of Akbar, was too powerless to prevent the coming dissolution. After him came Jahāndār Shāh, a weak-minded prince, who was murdered within a year of his accession, followed by Farrukh Siyar, a still more incapable ruler who met the same fate six years later in 1719. Two more of the same complexion came and went in the very same year. And then followed the gay and profligate puppet, Muḥammad Shāh, whose reign of nearly thirty years witnessed that great calamity and scourge, the invasion of India by the Persian tyrant Nādir Shāh and the sack of Delhi by him in 1739.

This event demonstrated, as nothing else had done since the death of Awrangzayb, that the Imperial dynasty had no effective hold on the country. It weakened beyond recovery what little central authority there was before, and emboldened not only the avowed enemies of the empire, but even ambitious Muslim governors of provinces to profit by the confusion. So, during the next reign of Aḥmad Shāh, one province after another seceded under some pretext or other, Bengal under 'Alī Wardī Khān, the Deccan under the Niẕāmu'l-Mulk, and Oudh under the Nawwāb Wazīr. The Mahrattas raised their head and extended the sphere of their mischief; so did the Rohillas from Rohilkhanḍ. The lesson was not lost on the Afghans too, who began to lay waste the Punjab.

Added to these troubles, the nobles at the central seat of government were growing more and more restive and rebellious, with the result that Aḥmad Shāh was deposed in 1754, and his successor, 'Ālamgīr II, murdered in 1759, and the heir-apparent, Shāh 'Ālam, finding his life in danger, fled to Bengal and sought the protection of the English East India Company, which had established its power there after the battle of Plassey in 1757. The throne of Delhi was vacant. The Mahrattas on the one hand, and the Afghans on the other, seized the opportunity and advanced towards Delhi, each anxious to usurp the sovereignty of the imperial city. The battle that was fought between them at Panipat near Delhi in 1761, although it shattered for ever the dreams of Mahratta ascendancy in North India, did not prevent them from repeating their depredations soon after the Afghans, owing to affairs in Afghanistan, had to retrace their steps, leaving desolate Delhi to look after itself. The claimant to the throne, Shāh 'Ālam, was still in exile. When he returned, however, to Delhi in 1764, after the battle of Buxor between the Nawwāb Wazīr and the English, he did so practically as a pensioner of the East India Company, on whom he had been obliged, by force of circumstances, to confer the Dīwānī or administration of Bengal, of which they were already in virtual possession.

From this time onward Delhi became the seat of pensioners who kept up a phantom court, and whose diminishing authority as "Emperors," did not extend much beyond the city of Delhi and its immediate vicinity. Even this did not last very long, for with the outbreak of the Indian Mutiny in 1857, and the trial and deportation of Bahādur Shāh Ẓafar, the last of the House of Tīmūr, what little influence and power the Muslims still enjoyed in Delhi came to a sudden and most inglorious end. Lucknow, the seat of the Nawwāb Wazīr of Oudh, which, during the declining years of the Court of Delhi, had welcomed and sheltered Muslim emigrants, particularly the literary class, from that city, had already disappeared in 1856, and there was now no place left in North India to which the Muslims could turn for refuge and support.[1] Bereft of power and wealth, and with nothing else to fall back upon in life, the Muslim community in North India presented, at the close of our period, a pathetic spectacle for which there are few parallels in the history of mankind.

Religious and Social.—Alongside of this decline in their political power, there was, during the period under review, a gradual disintegration of their religious and social life, which in no small measure contributed to their political downfall. The severe monotheism of Islam which their

[1] See also Introduction to *Gulshan-i-Hind*, Lahore, 1906.

early ancestors had brought with them into India, and its spirit of social democracy, had slowly given place to a crude anthropomorphism on the one hand, and to a hierarchical conception of society on the other, informed by the religious and social spirit of the Hindu community amidst whom they had lived for centuries together.

Religious.—The idea of one God, Transcendent, Omnipotent, and Merciful, and the conception of direct individual responsibility for human action which is so distinctive and fundamental a characteristic of Islam, was obscured in the popular mind by the observance of customs and practices resembling those prevalent among Hindus. The ignorance of the masses, and their superstition, was exploited by the priesthood in its own interests, and belief in the efficacy of charms and amulets, of spells and incantations, signs and omens, palmistry and astrology, and the punctilious observance of rites and ceremonies, came to occupy the place of religion in their daily life, while the more thoughtful and religious-minded fell under the influence of a special class of priests, who, as " Pīrs " or spiritual preceptors, initiated them into the mysteries of the esoteric life. This phase of philosophic Islam, known under the common name of " Ṣūfism," found a quite congenial soil in India, where the ascetic ideal and the disciplinary practices of the Yogīs were for long highly valued.

Thus the religion of Islam, which was at once so spiritual and practical, and which had awakened nations from age-long stupor, and vitalised and energised them, a religion which once stood for rationalism and progress, ceased under the influence of pharisaical priests, trading upon the credulity and ignorance of the masses, to be an inspiring and ennobling influence in their life. Not that some of these evils had not crept into the life of Muslim races before they came to India, but they became much more pronounced and general in this country, owing to the prevailing polytheism and the attendant rites and practices of Hindu society. The form was kept, while the spirit was lost, and even around this form, excrescences had grown which disfigured it almost beyond recognition.

Social.—Nor was it different in social life. The ideal of human equality and brotherhood, which was another basic principle of Islam, gradually gave place to the spirit of caste, and the organisation of society on that basis, which may be said to constitute the essence of Hindu religion. Sayyids came to be regarded on the score of their birth with special sanctity like the Brahmins; and other races, like the Turks and Afghans, and the mass of Indian converts were assigned their graded position in the social scale. Occupations like those of the sweeper, the butcher, and the fuller were stratified into so many castes on a more or less exclusive basis. Many of the customs relating to birth, marriage, and death, having no sanction either in Islamic theory or practice anywhere abroad, were adopted from the Hindus. Early marriages became more frequent, and widow marriages, allowed in Islam and common in other Islamic countries, were discouraged and even looked down upon in accordance with Hindu notions. The seclusion of women, only partially allowed by religion, became, partly in imitation of Rajput practice, and partly from considerations of pride and prestige, much more rigid in India than anywhere else. And the class of courtesans, who had a recognised and even an honoured place in Hindu society, came to be patronised by the richer classes of Muslims. Thus all the features of a corrupt and degenerate society were there. Power had brought wealth, wealth luxury, and with luxury all the evils which come in its train. Drunkenness and dissolution were rife. The Court set the fashion, and the courtiers and the higher classes of society followed the example. They forsook all manly games and sports, and indulged in such pastimes as cock and partridge fighting, hawking, pigeon-training and kite-flying. They disdained the pursuit of trade, commerce, or industry. Their mainstay was administration in its civil and military branches, and as they began to lose their political power in one part of the country after another, their economic condition grew steadily worse. The social evils remained, but the wealth to gratify them was no longer there.

The condition of Muslim society, therefore, whether viewed in its political, religious, or social aspect, was, during this period, one of gradual degeneration and decay. No living principle helped to sustain them in any sphere. The binding force of imperialism, and of a common racial or national consciousness, had disappeared, and in its place particularism in its various forms and with all its disruptive tendencies held sway. The inspiration, and guidance of religion were lost under the influence of sacerdotalism and sterile obscurantism. The principle of social democracy—of equality and brotherhood among the followers of a common faith—ceased to be a cementing bond, and its very antithesis, the division of society into more or less exclusive groups, was at work. The outlook was altogether dark and gloomy, and there was nothing in the life of the Muslims to clear and brighten it.

(ii) Limitations of the Poets

No wonder then that Urdu poetry, which took its rise in an atmosphere such as this, was uninspiring and lifeless. Nor was there anything in the life and training of the poets themselves to help them to rise above their environment and hold out to those around them a standard of thought and feeling which would have sustained them in their misfortunes and contributed to their moral and social regeneration. In the first place, their educational and intellectual training was a great obstacle in the way of any healthy literary production. They were mostly fed and nursed, like everyone else in that age having any sort of claim to literary training, on the then existing Persian poetry and on the literary ideals which it embodied. They considered it part of a liberal education to be thoroughly versed in all the intricacies of Persian prosody as it had been adopted from the Arabs. To follow this system in their writings and to imitate Persian poetry in almost every little detail was their one ambition. Nothing with them was entitled to the rank of literature which was not borne out by the example of some recognised Persian poet.[1] With such a mental background, therefore, to their literary life, it was not surprising that they hardly ever felt it desirable to shake off this guidance and pursue a new line of their own. In the second place, circumstances of their material life very rarely allowed them to cultivate an independent mind. Most of them lived on the bounty and munificence of either the Courts of Delhi and Lucknow or such members of the aristocracy as had any interest in literature. As this patronage, partly owing to the whims and idiosyncrasies of those who offered it, and partly to the vicissitudes which overtook them during this troublous period, was a fluctuating and uncertain element, the Muslim poets were never a prosperous class, who could have taken an independent attitude in literature. It is significant of the state of Muslim society that men like Mīr Taqī and Sayyid Inshā', great names in the early Urdu poetry, should have died in abject penury.[2] There was in those days no independent Press and no large class of independent reading public who could have afforded these poets the necessary recognition and calmness of mind so helpful in literary pursuits.

In these circumstances, the poets were obliged to conform to the taste of their patrons on whom they depended,

[1] See also Introduction to *Gulshan-i-Hind*, Lahore, 1906.

[2] See Āzād, *Āb-i-Ḥayāt*, Lahore, 1899. Also 'Abd[u] 'l-Qādır, *New Urdu Literature*, Lahore, 1898.

or of that small class of people who, from time to time, used to congregate, sometimes at their houses, sometimes at the residences of their patrons, and sometimes at the shrines of well-known saints, where "mushā'iras" or poetical contests after the fashion of the Persians were held. It was at these literary meetings that the poets usually read most of their compositions for the first time. A hemistich, or sometimes a distich was circulated beforehand to suggest the metre and the rhyme in which they were required to express their thoughts. There was no restriction as regards the choice of subject. The poet could indulge in a variety of themes, from the sublime to the most ridiculous, in one and the same poem. The aim was to say anything and everything which pleased the composer so long as it was set in the prescribed metre and rhyme. In a short *Ghazal* or ode of eight or ten lines, the poet was at liberty to dwell on as many different subjects, none of which need have any connection with the other. There were, however, certain limitations to this freedom. No subject was to be touched, no figure of speech employed, no idiom or even an illusion used which had not been used by one or other of the writers of the classical Persian poetry. For every little innovation they were asked to cite authority. Poetry thus became conventional and artificial. It aimed at nothing but clothing in Urdu the thought and imagery of Persian poetry.

(iii) Classification of Urdu Poetry

A classification of this Urdu poetry on any scientific lines is not easy, for it is very rarely that the Urdu poet adheres to his subject throughout his poem. Even while he is consciously attempting to write on any set theme, for example a love-story, he very often falls into such repeated digressions and introduces such a large quantity of irrelevant matter, mostly consisting of his own morbid reflections, that not only is the unity of the poem entirely lost, but the main subject thrown into the background. It is because of this, as well as in imitation of the Persians, that Urdu poets arrange their works (Dīwān), not according to the subject, but according to the verse forms they employ. There is a considerable variety of these, and no one is entitled to the name of a poet unless his works show specimens of all.

There are eighteen of these which are rather important. They may be grouped under two heads—one comprising those forms which, for some reason or other, have been given special names, the other, of those which derive their names by the number of lines in each stanza. Of the first, those which are largely in use are (1) *Ghazal*, or ode, a short poem usually of four to fifteen couplets, with the first, second, and every alternate line thereafter rhyming together; (2) *Qaṣīda*, or purpose-poem, of thirty to ninety-nine couplets, identical in form with the *Ghazal*; (3) *Qiṭa'*, or fragment, similar to *Qaṣīda*, but of unlimited length, and with the first two hemistichs not rhyming together; (4) *Naẓm*, same as Qiṭa', but beginning with a rhymed couplet; (5) *Masnawī*, or "double rhymed," resembling the rhymed couplet of Pope; (6) *Rubā'ī*, or quatrain, of the type of 'Umar-i-Khayyām; (7) *Tarjī'-Band*, or "Return Tie," consisting of a succession of stanzas in the same metre but with a different rhyme; and (8) *Tarkīb-Band*, or "Composite Tie," which differs from *Tarjī'-Band* in only certain minor details. The other group chiefly consists of (1) *Murabba'*, or Foursome, a poem employing a succession of four-line stanzas called *Band* or tie; (2) *Mukhammas*, or Fivesome; (3) *Musaddas*, or Sixsome; (4) *Musabba'*, or Sevensome; (5) *Muṣamman*, or Eightsome; (6) *Mutassa'*, or Ninesome; and (7) *Mu'ash-shar*, or Tensome.

It may be observed that these verse forms are capable

of an endless number of varieties according to the length of the line or the number of long and short or heavy or light syllables, and it is beyond the scope of our subject to describe them with any elaboration. Mention is made of them here only to show how Urdu poetry is hedged in and even lost in a maze of artificial verse forms, and how difficult it is to understand the spirit, substance, and characteristics of this poetry merely in terms of these forms.

We shall therefore attempt to classify Urdu poetry according to subject, in so far as it is susceptible of any such classification. At the very outset it may be definitely stated that the department of drama was absolutely untouched by the early Urdu poets. In fact they seem to have been quite ignorant of the existence of any such form of literature. Even if some of them were aware of the Sanskrit drama, they were precluded from exercising their poetical faculty in that direction, simply because none of the Persian poets had done so. With the elimination, therefore, of drama, all that we find in the early Urdu poetic literature is either lyrical or epic in substance.

The lyrical poetry in Urdu may be divided into four classes—Panegyric, Erotic, Didactic, and Elegiac.

Panegyric.—Most of the poets, as observed above, were dependent for their daily material comfort on the patronage of either the rulers of Delhi and Lucknow, or of the nobility who flourished at their Courts. It was not only the fashion of the day to compose panegyrics after the style of the Persians, but incumbent on them to praise their patrons to their face and extol their real or supposed virtues.

The form that lent itself easily to such a subject is the *Qaṣīda*. It consists of two parts. The first is known as *Nasīb*, or exordium; the second as *Maqṣūd*, or purpose. Very rarely was there any essential connection between the two, although in theory it was considered part of poetic art to dovetail the one into the other. The subject of the exordium might be anything—the season of the year in which the poem was composed, or any particular object which the patron held dear, such as his horse or sword, or some moral or philosophical reflection, or an account of the wretched condition of the poet himself. The second part dealt with the qualities of the head and heart of the patron in a grand and pompous style, embellished with gorgeous imagery borrowed from the Persian panegyrists. The picture was incomplete and not worthy of consideration if he was not represented as the embodiment of all possible virtues. He might in his real life have been one of the most worthless of men, but with the poet he was brave as Rustam or Isfandiyār, kind and merciful as ‘Alī, bountiful as Ḥātim, just as Farīdūn, magnificent as Jamshīd or Afrāsiyāb, powerful as Dārā or Sikandar (Alexander the Great), wise as Socrates or Aristotle, and so on. Some of these are the legendary heroes of Persia immortalised in the *Shāh Nāma* of Firdawsī, and the Urdu panegyrist seriously considered it his bounden duty to drag them into his compositions. Indeed, there was no limit to his extravagance; he would invest his patron with every noble virtue in order to please him. One poet vied with another in this art of flattery. The more novel the way, the louder the applause that the poet received from his hearers.

Of the panegyrists in Urdu, Sawdā and Sayyid Inshā’ once enjoyed the greatest popularity. It was they who brought this art to perfection. Indeed, a few of their compositions are considered to have surpassed, in their charm and style, even those of Anwarī and Khāqānī,[1] the Persian panegyrists who set the standard. Possibly so. But in spirit and substance the Urdu *Qaṣīdas* hardly deserve the name of serious literature.[2] They neither represent the real nor portray the ideal. One sometimes wonders whether the writers had any sense of decency and self-

[1] See *Āb-i-Ḥayāt.*

[2] See *Musaddas-i-Ḥālī.*

respect. Even a poet of the rank of G͟hālib, at whose feet the great Ḥālī, the leader of the new movement in Urdu poetry, began to " lisp in numbers," and who undoubtedly showed in some of his *G͟hazals* a spirit of independence such as his contemporaries or predecessors never possessed, even he fell a victim to the tastes and tendencies of his time. In some of his *Qaṣīdas* addressed to Bahādur Shāh, of whose tragic end after the Indian Mutiny reference has already been made, G͟hālib indulged in a string of such impossible similes, metaphors, and epithets, attributing to the feeble and helpless State pensioner powers which the mightiest of princes in modern times might blush to own.

Erotic.—The weaknesses which the panegyric poetry in Urdu represents—artificiality, conventionality, insincerity, and an abject dependence on Persian models—are to be seen in a more pronounced form in the next division of poetry, viz. the Erotic. It was in this more than in any other department of literature that the early Urdu poets could easily have afforded to strike out an independent line of their own. For the feeling of love is so intensely subjective that it does not require the aid of any artificial devices for its expression. Unfortunately, however, they would not listen to the natural dictates of the human heart, but most slavishly went out to the Persian poets for guidance as to what they should feel and how they should give expression to it. They pursued this strange course with such zeal and perseverance that they not only succeeded in vitiating the taste of their own age but have left behind a legacy, the temptation of which has proved too strong even for some of the lyrists of the present time, whose intellectual and literary training has been conducted largely on Western lines.

Urdu erotic poetry is most voluminous. The largest number of pages in the works of every poet are occupied by this. It is usually expressed in the form of *Ghazal* and deals with love in all its manifold aspects. Outwardly it is voluptuous and bacchanalian in character, but it has become a fashion to read behind its outward form some esoteric or Ṣūfistic meaning, as they do in Persia. Because of this spiritual significance, it is very popular and is held in great estimation by the Muslim community in India. In some of the writings of the leading poets, such as Mīr Dard, Mīr Taqī, Ẕawq and Ghālib, it presents a verbal charm considered hardly less fascinating than some of the best *Ghazals* in Persian poetry.[1] Still the fact remains, which may not be fully admitted by some of its modern advocates, that it is an extremely artificial poetry. Persian in conception, Persian in feeling, Persian in tone, Persian in imagery, and Persian even in local colouring, and Persian in its esoteric associations, the erotic poetry in Urdu lives on a few conventional ideas. Without any exaggeration it may be asserted that, shorn of grammatical links, the voluminous literature of Urdu *Ghazals* may be reduced to a definite number of stereotyped phrases and words which are repeated from one *Ghazal* to another and by one poet after another. Because of the innumerable varieties of metric and of rhyme arrangements to which *Ghazal* lends itself, this poverty of ideas and of feeling may not be easily discernible. But a careful analysis will at once show the truth of the contention.

The literature of the *Ghazal* had, during the period under review, a deadening influence on the Muslim community. More than any political event it contributed to their degeneration. Its bacchanalian tendencies and suggestions impaired their moral character. Its Ṣūfistic ideal, instead of purifying their spiritual life, drove not a few among them to the camp of the professional beggar and the ascetic, and its gospel of pessimism gave them a wrong outlook on life and suppressed every desire for material progress. It

[1] See *Āb-i-Ḥayāt*, Lahore, 1899.

was not until the dawn of the new ideals from the West that the serious minded among the Muslim community realised what an unwholesome influence the *Ghazal* had had on their mind and character.[1]

Didactic.—The didactic poetry in Urdu scarcely presents any better spectacle. It consists mostly of satires which very rarely rise above the standard of lampoons and personal gibes and recriminations. The most outstanding name in this field of literature is that of Mīrzā Rafī'u 's-Sawdā', a writer whose mental condition, as described by the late Muḥammad Ḥusayn Āzād, strongly reminds one of Alexander Pope.[2]

Epic and Elegiac.—The narrative form of poetry occupies a place in Urdu literature next in importance only to the erotic. It is usually written in the verse form known as *Maṣnawī*, or " double rhyme," and consists very largely of love stories. The subject thus being love, the *Masnawī* is materially not very different from the *Ghazal* in its substance and poetic imagery. The most well-known and widely read *Maṣnawīs* are the *Badr-i-Munīr* of Mīr Ḥasan, and the *Gulzār-ī-Nasīm* of Pundit Dayā Shankar. The aim in these poems is not so much the development of action of the story or the delineation of character of the hero and other personages introduced in it, as the expression of the poet's own personal observations on the different aspects of human life. For this reason a large majority of the *Maṣnawīs* might as well be classified under the reflective or elegiac form of poetry. The same might be said of that large class of narrative poems by Dabīr and Anīs, called *Marṣiyas*, dealing with the tragedy of Karbalā and the massacre of the family of the Holy Prophet. It must be mentioned that elegies, properly so called, expressing sorrow over the loss of a personal friend or a national hero, were rarely

[1] See also Ḥālī's *Musaddas*, Delhi, 1886. Also Ḥāfiz Naẕīr Aḥmad, *On the Present State of Education among Muhammadans*, Agra, 1889.

[2] For an account of Sawdā's life, see *Āb-i-Ḥayāt*, Lahore, 1883.

attempted by the early Urdu poets. They contented themselves instead with writing short chronograms, a form of writing which hardly deserves to be treated as literature.

(iv) Recapitulation

Such, in brief outline, is the scope and character of the Urdu literature of the period under review. To recapitulate, it was wholly or almost wholly in verse. Prose had not yet been evolved, as Persian still continued to supply the need for it. This literature was thus entirely poetical in purpose, and was essentially subjective in character. The objective note was absent from it. Even the subjective element was of a highly artificial and conventional type. The ideals which it represented or embodied were unsuited to the production of creative literature. In consequence it failed or neglected to hold out to the world at large any living or inspiring message. In fact it went a long way to demoralise and vitiate the taste of those among whom it took its rise.

Still this literature had its own strong point. It fulfilled one good purpose, and that was that in a short period of about 150 years it succeeded, as probably no other literature has done, to form the language through which it expressed itself. It is to the untiring efforts of the poets of the decadent age of artificial poetry we have reviewed that the perfection of Urdu as a vehicle of literary expression is due. That is a distinct service which can hardly be overlooked. The early poets may thus be regarded as those who came to prepare the language for the easy assimilation of the influences and ideals which began to flow into it with the establishment of British rule in India, and which will form the subject of our study in the following chapters.

PART II

CHANNELS OF ENGLISH INFLUENCE

CHAPTER III

CHANNELS OF ENGLISH INFLUENCE

(i) Channels wholly English

In dealing with the influence of the West, which, as suggested in the preceding chapters, has profoundly affected Indian thought and literature in modern times, it is necessary to point out, at the very outset, that this influence has flowed into the country and made itself felt entirely under British rule and chiefly through English literature. This should be clearly borne in mind, lest the fact of India having also had connection during the last 300 years with other European nations besides the English, viz. the Portuguese, the Dutch, and the French, give rise to the thought that they also might have contributed in some measure to the dissemination of Western ideas in India and have influenced its literature.

It must be remembered that the contact of the Portuguese or the Dutch or the French with India was hardly of a nature calculated to create any deep impression on the life of the people. In the first place, their activity was short-lived and confined to small strips of territory mainly along the coast of Southern India. None of them had any direct relations with the people of the north, particularly with that section among whom Urdu language and literature grew and flourished. In the second place, the objects which they set before themselves were not likely to dispose even those owning immediate allegiance to them, whether through curiosity or admiration or necessity, to interest themselves in the thought and literature of their rulers. The Portuguese, who were the first to land on the shores of India, made themselves repugnant to the people from the beginning. Their lust of power and dominion and their religious fanaticism and forcible conversions never allowed them to exercise any salutary influence on those over whom they held their authority. The Dutch, who were the next to come from Europe, owing to their misfortunes at home, never made any headway in India and speedily sank into insignificance. The French, whose advent coincided roughly with that of the English, made, no doubt, an earnest bid for power and influence, but their inordinate ambition led to their undoing. They have left nothing behind in the form of thought or expression except hazy memories of their fitful intrigues against the rising power of the East India Company.

It will thus be seen that neither the French nor the Portuguese, much less the Dutch, had the time or the desire to stand as the exponents of Western learning and culture before the people of India. The Dutch have now permanently vanished from the scene. The Portuguese and the French still linger on, relegated to but tiny specks of land on the coast covering not more than a few square miles each, the former at Goa, Diu and Daman, and the latter at Pondicherry and Chandernagore, from where, whatever their usefulness to those who acknowledge their authority, they have scarcely any chance of exercising any cultural influence on the vast millions of the great continent from which they are practically shut out.

It may therefore be safely assumed that all that we may discern in Urdu or, for the matter of that, in any other Indian literature, as belonging to the West, has come in almost entirely through English agencies, the most important of which has been English literature. Because of this enormous share which English has taken in the spread of Western thought in India, we may with every justification speak of Western influence in Urdu literature as the influence of English literature *par excellence.*

(ii) Channels Classified and Described

Before we proceed to examine the nature of this influence, it would be necessary to describe the main channels and agencies through which it has exerted itself upon the minds of the people and found expression in their literature. These may be classified broadly into four kinds, all linked together in their natural growth and formation, and all moving along with a common purpose by correcting or modifying or supplementing the activity of one another.

In the first place there is the atmosphere itself created in the country by the establishment of a uniform and centralised system of enlightened and modern administration under the ægis of the British Crown, an atmosphere charged with all those ideas and conceptions which are usually associated with the West, especially England. Secondly, as a natural result of British administration, there has come into being a governmental system of education essentially Western and scientific in preference to the indigenous and Oriental classical learning, and based upon English both as a language and as a medium of instruction in all subjects. In the carrying on of this system the efforts of Government have been aided and supplemented by voluntary organisations, missionary (Christian) or national, which have conformed to the curricula, standards, and methods of instruction laid down by Government or by quasi-governmental institutions such as the Universities of the different provinces. Thirdly, as a distinct and spontaneous expression of the reaction to Western thought generated by the widespread system of Western education, have arisen various movements, political, social and religious, which in their several ways have served as *further* channels of the new ideas among the people. Lastly, by way of complement to all these activities, has come the

Press, English and vernacular, which has gradually increased in power and usefulness in forming and educating public opinion on modern lines.

(iii) The Atmospheric Influence

To take these one by one, it should first be noticed what the advent of English power actually meant to the people of India. With the decline and disintegration of the Mogul Empire following the death of Awrangzayb, there was, as shown in the preceding chapter, absolutely no central authority in the country. During the whole of the eighteenth century and part of the nineteenth, India was in a state of continuous turmoil, confusion and anarchy. It can easily be imagined what an unsettling effect such a state of affairs must have produced on the minds of the people and what a considerable relief it must have been to them to see some strong well-organised power emerging out of the chaos and consciously assuming the rôle of the restorer of peace and order in the country. That fact affords the real secret of the success which attended the work of the English East India Company. The masses never stopped to inquire whether this rising power was alien or indigenous. To them "it was immaterial as to who ruled over them, whether Rama or Ravana," as the Indian saying goes, so long as they were left to live in peace. It was, however, different with the higher classes, who with the spread of British dominion were gradually losing their authority and influence among the people. For a time they formed the chief source of discontent and disaffection which culminated in the outbreak of the great Sepoy rebellion in 1857. Its suppression marked the termination of that long period of disorder and confusion which had followed the downfall of the Mogul Empire.

With 1858 there dawned a new era in the country, an

era of peace and prosperity. The rule of a trading body who naturally used to look more to the interests of their shareholders than to the welfare of those under its charge was now over. The English East India Company was abolished, and the responsibility of administration taken over by the Crown. This change of hands was but an expression of a change in the conception of Government. For the first time in the annals of British connection with India, it was declared that the "contentment of the people and their happiness and prosperity"[1] was the chief aim of the rulers. New and modern administrative standards were set up, and the functions of Goverment, hitherto limited to the primary duties of justice, police and revenue, were considerably enlarged. Not only was the administrative machinery thoroughly overhauled and reconstructed, but new departments were opened both in the Imperial and Provincial Governments for meeting the ever-growing needs of the people. In fact the whole apparatus of modern civilised administration came into existence, which with the advance of time has gone on increasing in efficiency, offering to the people of the soil greater and greater opportunities of association and direction.

This change in the aim and policy of Government and the moral and material improvement it has worked since its inception, has succeeded in creating an entirely new atmosphere in the country which has gradually awakened the people to a sense of the needs and requirements of modern life and acquainted them with the principles and standards of modern administration as understood in England.

[1] See Queen Victoria's Proclamation, 1858.

(iv) The Educational System [1]

More important than this atmospheric influence generated by the improved and modern methods of government, has been the specific influence exerted upon the minds of the people by the system of education established in the country. To trace the early history of this system or the steps by which the British Government slowly came to recognise the education of the people as part of its administrative functions is beyond the scope of this chapter. Nor would such an attempt be profitable from the point of view of Urdu literature. For the Indian Muslims, among whom this literature has grown and flourished, did not interest themselves in any particular manner in the educational activity of the Government, and in fact tacitly held aloof from it until the system was in full working order. It is sufficient to point out here that by the time the Muslims, having received a rude awakening by the Great Indian Mutiny, realised the necessity of marching with the times and participating in the governmental system of education so far monopolised by the Hindus for whom it was originally designed, the period, first of reluctance by the British Government to interest themselves in the education of the people, and then of controversy as regards the nature of instruction to be imparted, whether on Western or Oriental lines, had long passed away. By the year 1859, the Government was committed definitely to a system of education carried on by means of schools and colleges and universities fashioned on English models and providing instruction in

[1] For an account of the successive stages in the educational policy of the British Government in India leading to the establishment of the system under reference see the following:—

Arthur Howell, *Education in British India prior to* 1854.
Trevelyan, *On the Education of the People of India.*
Trevelyan, *Life of Macaulay*, ed. 1881.
Edinburgh Review, "Indian Missions," 1808.
Report of the Indian Education Commission, 1882.

Western sciences, arts, history, philosophy and literature through the medium of the English language.

It must be observed that the demand for such a system of education did not originate with the Government, although they ultimately realised the need for it, but came from private agencies such as the several Christian Missions established in the country, who had in fact anticipated and, in a way, even prepared the ground for its establishment, and from the Hindu intelligentsia, themselves the products of missionary education, at the head of whom was Rāja Rām Mohan Roy, founder of the new eclectic creed of Bramo-Samāj. The Indian Muslims, obsessed with the sense of their own self-importance, and impotently disdainful of the encroachment of Western thought into a country where they had held the mastery for several centuries together, remained sullenly indifferent. Neither profiting by what was liberal and wholesome in their own Islamic training, nor willing to recognise the good in what the new system offered, they let the Hindus steal a march on them until there arose among them a man with a large vision and foresight who made it his life-work to fight against this apathy and bring back his co-religionists to the path of progress and enlightenment. The writings of Sir Sayyid Aḥmad and of the small band of workers who made it a common cause with him to give a new life and a new outlook to their community will be noticed later on as the first expression in Urdu literature of that reaction to Western thought which had already begun to manifest itself in the activity and literature of the Hindus. Suffice it to mention here that since his trumpet call first went round, there has come about a great change in the attitude of the Muslims towards Western education. The Muhammadan Anglo-Oriental College at Aligarh founded by Sir Sayyid Aḥmad in 1876, now grown into a statutory residential and teaching University, and similar Muslim institutions though on a smaller scale established in different parts of India, the steadily increasing influx of Muslim youth into Government and other non-denominational colleges and schools all over the country, and the inauguration a few years ago of the Osmania University at the capital of the premier Muslim State of Hyderabad, bear unmistakable testimony to the response which the Muslim community in India has so far made to this new system.

As a result, in common with their Hindu compatriots, the Muslim educated classes have had, during the last half-century, an ever-widening scope and opportunity for the study of Western sciences, arts, philosophy and literature. In this scheme of education, English has occupied a peculiarly important place. An acquaintance with it has formed an indispensable preliminary to the acquisition of modern knowledge. It has been the only medium of instruction in almost every subject from the lowest stage in secondary school education to the highest in the University. For this reason and for the fact that the University courses of study have been heavily loaded with English language and literature, they have had to devote to this subject greater time and attention than to any other, including their own vernaculars. In consequence, whatever their individual interest in any particular branch of knowledge, they have been obliged to make English literature a special feature of their education, and to acquaint themselves not merely with the writings of the leading English poets and prose writers, their mind and art, but with the various movements, political, social, religious, literary, intellectual or æsthetic, of which these writers have either been the spokesmen or the products. As the study of English literature would, however, be incomplete without a reference to the different influences from the Continent which have affected its development, they have had necessarily, though in the majority of cases in a casual manner, to acquaint themselves, primarily through English translations, with the literary models and ideals not only of classic Greece and Rome but also of modern Europe. Thus it is that the system of Governmental education established in the country with its great emphasis on the study of English language and literature, has opened out to the Indian mind a boundless treasure-house of large and inspiring ideas and ideals which we are accustomed to associate with the healthier and nobler side of English life and English culture.

(v) Religious, Social and Political Movements

Religious and Social.—The first results of this new training were felt, as was indeed anticipated and foreseen by its promoters long ago,[1] in a natural desire on the part of those imbued with the new ideas to apply them to the improvement of the religious, social and political condition of their own country. The Hindus were the first to enter the field, as was natural under the circumstances. Centuries of political subjection and age-long acquiescence in a degrading social order and submission to the religious domination of Brahminic priesthood had left them in greater need of some quickening influence which might set them free. When, therefore, with the establishment of peace and order in the country, the necessary awakening came to them from the West by means of Western education to which they had so kindly taken from the beginning, the more thoughtful and earnest minds among them naturally felt a strong inclination to seek freedom from the social and religious shackles which had bound them so long. Some there were among these who were bold enough to welcome all that was of good report from any source whatsoever, whether Christianity or

[1] See Charles Grant's *Observations on the State of Society among the Asiatic Subjects in Great Britain, particularly with Respect to Morals; and on the Means of Improving it*, 1792; Parliamentary Papers relating to the Affairs of India: *General*, Appendix I; *Public* (1832), pp. 3–89. Also Maucalay's Minute in Favour of English Education, 1835.

Hinduism or Islam, or any philosophic system of the East or West, so long as it contributed to their moral and social welfare. That was the attitude reflected and embodied in the Bengali movement of *Brahmo-Samāj*. There were, however, those who were not able to go so far and in fact were hardly in sympathy with the heterodox tendencies of the *Bramo-Samāj*, but were at the same time alive to the need of arresting the tide of scepticism which was passing over their intellectuals, which could not, however, be satisfied unless the Hindu faith were remoulded to suit the requirements of modern life. Not willing to introduce reform merely in the name of the new ideas from the West, and at the same time finding not much inspiration from the prevailing religion, they looked back into the dim and distant past, to the time when Hindu society was still in the primitive stage and Hindu religion was but a simple creed unencumbered by later Brahminic additions, and tried to seek for some semblance of authority for any change they contemplated in their religious and social life. This was the disposition which found expression in the establishment of the *Āryā-Samāj* and the *Sanātana Dharma*. Midway between these two, between the eclecticism of *Brahmo-Samāj* and the orthodoxy of *Sanātana Dharma*, there have arisen a few schools of thought like the Theosophical, which represent compromises in varying degrees.

The same feeling for religious and social reform was also felt among the Muslim community. Prominent among those who associated themselves with this movement among the Muslims were Sir Sayyid Aḥmad of Aligarh and Mīrzā G͟hulām Aḥmad of Qādiyān, representing each a particular section of the community. Opinions may differ as to how far these reformers received their stimulus from the new ideas of the West Indeed the followers of Mīrzā G͟hulām Aḥmad would even suggest absolute divine inspiration underlying the activity of their religious leader. Still, making all allowance for honest belief, the broad fact remains that these reformers were, as their writings indicate. undeniably the products, direct or indirect, of those influences from the West which, as the result of English administration and English education, were spreading all over the country.

Political.—The same has to be said of the political movements which arose in the wake of the establishment of the new educational system. In this sphere, as in that of the social and religious, the Hindus were again the first to take the initiative. The ideas of freedom and democracy for which England has avowedly stood since the beginning of the nineteenth century, and which the study of Mill and Burke in the Universities had transmitted to the Indian students, could not but react on their pliable minds. They engendered in them a growing feeling for political advancement, a feeling which found expression in the several organisations which the English educated class among the Hindus founded in different parts of the country, like the *Mahājana Sabhā* in Madras, the Presidency Association in Bombay, the *Sarvajanik Sabhā* in Poona and the Indian National Congress.

The Muslims were rather slow to move in politics and were not able to fall into line with the Hindus until very recently. Their immediate and primary need was modern education. So, while the others were striving to get more and more voice in the administration, the Muslims, led by Sir Sayyid Aḥmad and with the help of the All-India Muhammadan Educational Conference and its auxiliary agencies, devoted themselves exclusively to the cause of Muslim education. Till the beginning of this century they had absolutely no idea of directly associating themselves with the political movements of the country. In fact they viewed them with suspicion and distrust. They preferred to let the English govern rather than help their erstwhile subjects, the Hindus, to rule over them. Such an attitude could not, however, last long. They saw how from day to day the British Goverment were gradually giving way to the clamour of the Hindu politicians. They were thus forced to realise that they would be left considerably behindhand in the race of life if they did not bestir themselves and march with the current. Thus came into existence the All-India Muslim League in 1908 and its affiliated associations, which, though started as defensive political organisations, were by the pressure of events forced in 1916 to identify themselves with the aims and aspirations of the Indian National Congress.

(vi) Press

As a complement to all these movements, and as a necessary feature of modern life, has come the Indian Press, which has contributed in no small measure to the spread of the new ideas among a much wider public than any of the other channels mentioned above has been capable of reaching.

The history of this Press goes back indeed to the days of Hastings and Cornwallis. But for a long time its scope was very limited. It was owned and edited by Englishmen for the benefit of the small colony of English residents stationed either at the provincial capitals or in the interior of the country. After the Indian Mutiny, however, this Press entered upon a quite new existence. The improvement of communications within the country by means of roads, railways and telegraphs, and with Europe, particularly after the opening of the Suez Canal, contributed materially to its efficiency as a news agency, and the large influx of Europeans into the country in different capacities, as well as the rise of a new class of intelligentsia, the products of the newly established Universities, greatly increased its circulation. It also assumed, as a consequence, its legitimate function of directing and educating public opinion. But its views did not always find favour with the politically minded class of English educated Indians, who naturally felt the need of having organs of their own. As a result, a number of newspapers and periodicals were started in English in different provinces by Indians, who, however, soon realised the limitations of such an English Press in a country where the vast majority of the people were ignorant of the language. For while it fulfilled a very useful and necessary purpose in moulding Indian opinion along certain well-defined lines, and acquainting the Government with the aims and aspirations of the people as understood by the English educated class, it could not reach the masses and serve as a lever for their social uplift. Hence arose the vernacular Press, to which increasing attention has been paid in recent years by the leaders of Indian thought, both Hindu and Muslim, and which has steadily grown in power and in usefulness.

This vernacular Press includes a large number of periodicals and covers a wider range of topics than the English Press. While not neglecting political questions, it has devoted special attention to social, religious and literary subjects, and has thus been instrumental in conveying, in however simple and crude a manner, to the Indian public at large, practically all the ideas symbolised by Western education.

(vii) Conclusion

Thus, in these several ways, through an improved form of British administration, through the new system of Western education and the various movements which it has given rise to, as well as through the Press, the lives and thoughts of the people have been profoundly influenced by the new ideas and impulses which have come from the West. The cumulative result has been something phenomenal. Seldom in the history of the world, in modern times, has any country been exposed to such a sudden and lurid glare of vitalising ideas and conceptions. The nearest approach to this is perhaps the Renaissance in Europe, of which these ideas are themselves largely the outcome. Indeed in many respects the present movement in India is a much more powerful one. For, however great the share which the Renaissance ultimately had in the creation of Modern Europe, we should not forget that in its early stages it was comparatively a very unassuming movement. It was not, like the modern awakening in India, the result of the *living* contact of one race and culture with another; it was merely a rediscovery of the neglected and long-forgotten literature and art of an almost extinct people. Nor was it so comprehensive in its scope, embracing nearly every sphere of human activity, nor did it operate over so wide an area or over so vast a population, nor again did it possess all those facilities which exist in these days for the wide and rapid dissemination of its ideas.

The change in India would have been much greater had this movement taken rise among a less heterogeneous people at a more or less common level of culture. As it is, people in the most varying degrees of civilisation, from the highest to the lowest, have been brought under its influence. The result has not therefore been uniform. Even in classes that have reacted most, the influence has not been as deep as one would expect. For the old order still continues to exist side by side with the new. As men cannot entirely cut themselves off from the past, the new ideas have necessarily not had the fullest freedom. This fact should therefore be clearly kept in mind when we come to review their results in the field of literature.

PART III

RESULTS OF ENGLISH INFLUENCE

CHAPTER IV

SPIRIT OF REVOLT OR REACTION AGAINST OLD LITERARY IDEALS

(i) The Aligarh Movement

The first effect on Urdu of the influence of Western thought as represented in English literature was manifested in the spirit of dissatisfaction with the traditional literary ideals which had so far been in vogue among the Urdu-speaking section of the Indian population. This dissatisfaction, it may be pointed out, was not voiced by any body of literary men deeply versed in English literature or whose early education and training were conducted exclusively on English lines, but by men such as Sayyid Aḥmad, Muḥammad Shiblī Nu'mānī, and Muḥammad Ḥusayn Āzād, whose formative period of life was spent in purely Eastern surroundings and in the pursuit of Eastern knowledge, and most of whom came under English influences only in their middle or advanced age. Still, such was their mind and genius, such their receptive capacity, that they never held themselves slaves to authority and tradition, but were willing to accept all that was of good report from wherever it came, and their one motto in life, as the opening pages of some of their writings bore, was in the words of their Prophet, "*Khuẕ mā ṣafā wa dā' mā Kadar,*" "Take that which is pure, discard that which is impure."

The most outstanding figure in this circle was Sayyid Aḥmad Khān, whose part in the socio-political movement of Aligarh we have already noticed in a previous chapter. Born in 1817 into a Sayyid family of Delhi, which for long had held positions of trust at the Mogul Court, he had from his childhood unique opportunities to watch and ruminate over the emptiness which surrounded the pomp and the "rule" of the "Emperors," and he foresaw that one day even this rule, such as it was, would disappear, leaving the Muslim community in abject helplessness. His father was a religious recluse. His early education was therefore conducted entirely under the guidance of his mother, a daughter of Khwāja Farīdu'd-Dīn, for long in the employ of the East India Company, as "attache to the Embassy sent in 1799 by Lord Wellesley to Persia," and as Political Officer at the Court of Ava, and who during the childhood of Sayyid Aḥmad was holding the place of Prime Minister to the "Emperor" of Delhi. The boy Sayyid Aḥmad did not study English at school. But the intimacy and friendship which existed between his family and the British Resident, General Ochterlony, who was "in the habit of visiting them at all hours of the day and night," [1] must have contributed in some measure to the development of his youthful mind. At all events, his admiration for English life and culture began from his boyhood, so much so that when his father, Sayyid Muḥammad Taqī, died in 1836, Sayyid Aḥmad, then only nineteen years old, chose, "much against the inclination of his relatives," to enter "the British Service as Sar-rishta-dār of the Criminal Department in the Ṣadr Amīn's office at Delhi," rather than accept the royal favours and enjoy the titles offered to him by the then Mogul "Emperor."

His rise from the humble position of Sar-rishta-dār to that of Subordinate Judge at Bijnore, his great services to the British Government during the time of the Indian Mutiny, his memorable visit to England in 1869 with his two sons, his meetings there with distinguished statesmen and men of letters, including Carlyle, who "was unusually gracious

[1] See G. F. J. Graham, *The Life and Work of Sir Sayyid Aḥmad Khān*, London, 1909.

to him," and with whom he "talked long and earnestly over *Heroes and Hero-Worship*, especially about Muḥammad," and his return to India with his mind vastly expanded, are described in some detail by his friend and biographer, Major-General G. F. J. Graham.[1]

The Aligarh movement which he launched and led until his death in 1898, and which found its great expression in the establishment in 1875 of the Muhammadan Anglo-Oriental College at Aligarh, now a statutory residential University, embodied the spirit which Sayyid Aḥmad had imbibed from Europe. As this spirit, which was reflected in every branch of its activity, has eventually manifested itself in Urdu literature, it appears necessary to indicate at this stage its broad features by way of introduction to what we have to discuss in the following pages. We will let Sayyid Aḥmad himself explain this spirit. Addressing Lord Lytton while laying the foundation of the M.A.O. College at Aligarh, he said:

"The British rule in India is the most wonderful phenomenon the world has ever seen. That a race living in a distant region, differing from us in language, in manners, in religion—in short, in all that distinguishes the inhabitants of one country from those of another—should triumph over the barriers which nature has placed in its way, and unite under one sceptre the various peoples of this vast continent, is in itself wonderful enough. But that they who have thus become the masters of the soil should rule its inhabitants, not with those feelings and motives which inspired the conquerors of the ancient world, but should make it the first principle of their government to advance the happiness of the millions of a subject race, by establishing peace, by administering justice, by spreading education, by introducing the comforts of life which modern civilisation has bestowed upon mankind, is to us manifestation of the hand of Providence, and an assurance of long life to the union of India with England.

[1] General Graham deals specially with the early life and work of Sayyid Aḥmad. For a fuller account of him after his return from England, see Ḥālī, *Ḥayāt-i-Jāwīd*, Cawnpore, 1901.

E

"To make these facts clear to the minds of our countrymen, to educate them so that they may be able to appreciate these blessings, to *dispel* those illusory traditions of the past which have hindered our progress, to *remove* those prejudices which have hitherto exercised a baneful influence on our race, to reconcile Oriental learning with Western literature and science, to inspire in the dreamy minds of the people of the East the practical energy which belongs to those of the West; to make the Mussalmans of India worthy and useful subjects of the British Crown; to inspire in them that loyalty which springs, not from servile submission to a foreign rule, but from genuine appreciation of the blessings of good government—these are the objects which the founders of the college have prominently in view. And looking at the difficulties which stood in our way, and the success which has already been achieved, we do not doubt that we shall continue to receive, even in larger measure, both from the English Government and from our own countrymen, that liberal support which has furthered our scheme, so that from the seed which we sow to-day there may spring up a mighty tree, whose branches, like those of the banyan of the soil, shall in their turn strike firm roots into the earth, and themselves send forth new and vigorous saplings; that this college may expand into a university, whose sons shall go forth throughout the length and breadth of the land to preach the gospel of free inquiry, of large-hearted toleration, and of pure morality."

(ii) Nature of Literary Reaction

The work of the Aligarh movement was in the beginning necessarily of the nature of propaganda, which led Sayyid Aḥmad and those who co-operated with him to examine the capacity of their language and literature as a vehicle of expression and as a means of catching the imagination of people and transmitting to them a little of the light which they had themselves received from the West. The standards which they brought to bear on this examination were the standards of English literature. The more they looked into it, the stronger did the conviction grow in them that their literature lacked in essentials, and stood in need of as much purification as the society itself which had fostered it.

It will be interesting to note the first impressions they formed of their own literature and the weaknesses it revealed under the searchlight of English literary ideals, as they will afford us an idea of the particular features of English literature which specially appealed to them and which they were anxious to assimilate and incorporate into their own.

In the preface to the *Nayrang-i-Khiyāl*, Muḥammad Ḥusayn Āzād, after lamenting the poverty of ideas in Urdu literature of his time, makes the following observation in regard to its style :

"The English language abounds with love subjects, tales and works of fiction. But the style (of these compositions) is something very different (from that of Urdu). The fundamental principle underlying it is that anything that is described should be done in such a way that the picture should rise before the mind's eye, and that its point should strike the heart. Hence (the English writers) apply to the branches only so many imaginary flowers and leaves as naturally suit the original, and not (so many) as will obscure the tree and branches altogether, presenting nothing but a heap of leaves."

Hāfiz Nazīr Aḥmad, another pioneer of the new movement, thus speaks of the injurious effects of the early literature on the morals of his community :

"The evils which beset us 'as a nation,' [1] though not all, at all events a great majority of them have been created by this literature. This literature teaches us falsehood and flattery. This literature suppresses and wipes out the real beauty of facts. This literature holds up baseless hypotheses and conjectures as 'facts.' This literature excites unwholesome passions. If anybody has merely tasted this poison, I have drunk it. If anybody has merely fondled it, I have let it bite me. Although in an advanced age I had, like an old parrot, a little smattering of English, the

[1] Note that the writer has used the English expressions "as a nation" and "facts" in the original Urdu.

colour of Asiatic learning had already stained my nature. However, this much must be admitted that thanks to this study of English I have gradually come to realise the defects of our literature." [1]

The poet, Sayyid Alṭāf Ḥusayn Ḥālī, the founder of the New School of Poetry, and indeed the greatest name in modern Urdu literature, has in the introduction to his famous elegiac poem, "The Flow and Ebb of Islam," *Madd wa Jazr-i-Islām*, given an account of the revulsion of feeling which came to him at the age of forty against all that he had so far written in the traditional style, the outstanding features of which, such as artificiality, conventionality, and insincerity, have already been noticed in a previous chapter. A passage from this introduction, in which he sums up the staple ideas on which the Urdu poets have always tirelessly harped in their poetic compositions, and which contributed so much to the conventional and artificial nature of their utterance, is worth reproducing here. In a spirit of sincere contrition he admits that he himself was in his earlier days a prey to these ideas. He says:

"Thanks to (this) poetic art, I had to play the conventional lover for some time. In the pursuit of an imaginary beloved I wandered for years over desert and wilderness and raised such a cloud of dust from under my feet that I defiled with it even Qays and Farhād.[2] Sometimes I shook a quarter of the inhabited world by my wailings. Sometimes I drowned the universe in the deluge of my eyes; made the angels deaf by the noise of my lamentations. The world screamed at the outpourings of my complaints. The Sky [3] got perforated by the rapid discharge (of the arrows) of my taunts. When convulsions of jealousy seized me, I considered the entire handiwork of God as my rival: indeed I grew suspicious even of myself. When the ocean

[1] See Lecture on *Musalmānān kī Ḥālat-i-Ta'līm*, Agra, 1889.

[2] Qays or Majnūn, the lover of Layla, and Farhād or Kohkan, the lover of Shīrīn, were celebrated in Arabic and Persian poetry, respectively.

[3] In Urdu poetry, as in Persian, the sky stands for God or Destiny

of my desire swelled, my heart's attraction did the work of magnetism. Often I enjoyed martyrdom by the sword of (the beloved's) eyebrows, and often did I regain life by her kicks, so much so, that life appeared but a garment which I took off or put on whenever it pleased me. Often did I visit the field of Judgment or Resurrection. Often did I stroll through Heaven and Hell. When the mood for drinking wine came upon me, jar after jar was rolled away empty; and withal there was no satiety. Sometimes I pressed my forehead on the threshold of a tavern, sometimes begged at the door of a wine-seller. Was pleased with unbelief; disliked faith; swore fealty to the chief priest of the Magi; became the disciple of Brahmins; worshipped idols; wore the Brahminic thread; applied the caste mark, reviled the pious; ridiculed the preacher; showed respect to the monastery and the house of idols; scoffed at the K'aba and the mosque; grew insolent to God; showed arrogance to prophets; regarded the miracles of Christ as a mere play, and the beauty of Joseph as but a show. Whenever I delivered a *G͟hazal*, I used the language of a rake; whenever a *Qaṣīda*, I made the jester and the professional flatterer open their mouth wide with wonder. In every pinch of dust I showed the properties of the elixir; in every dry stick the wonders of the rod of Moses. Of every Nimrod of the day I forged relations with Abraham. I let every helpless Pharaoh collide with Almighty God. Whoever I praised, I raised so high that the praised could hardly feel pleased with the praise. In a word, I blackened the book of my deeds so much that I did not leave even a speck of whiteness in it.

"When, on the day of Judgment, my sins would be inquired into,
The record of the sins of the world will be torn to pieces."

From the age of twenty to that of forty I revolved, like the oil-presser's bull, round the same circle and fancied that I had travelled all over the world. *When my eyes were, however, opened, I found I was still at the same place from which I had started.*" [1]

In the poem from the introduction to which we have quoted this somewhat lengthy passage, Hālī reverts to the subject and in a tone of deep indignation holds the early

[1] Special translation.

poetry as chiefly responsible for not only the decadence of learning among his people, but for their social and religious disintegration as well.[1] Never thereafter did Hālī attempt a love poem, never a line in the old conventional style.

> "I have done matching my voice with the nightingale in the garden;
> I have done reciting verses in the conclave of poets;
> Since thou hast forsaken me, O lively heart of my youth,
> I too have forsaken thy interminable stories."[2]

---

[1] 1. Special translation.

[2] *Quatrains of Ḥālī*, by G. E. Ward, Oxford, 1904.

CHAPTER V

NEW FORMS AND TECHNIQUE—VERSE

(i) Reasons for Dealing with Verse Separately from Prose

The literary revolt to which we have referred in the preceding chapter was accompanied by a desire to lay the foundation of a new literature in Urdu by employing it in wholly untried channels informed by the spirit and models of English literature. The task was by no means an easy one, for the literary taste of the people had grown as hardened as the social evils, and it was as difficult to purify the one as it was to eradicate the other. Still, thanks to the efforts of the pioneers of this movement and those who are carrying on their work at the present day, there has come into existence a voluminous literature of a new type, infinitely more bulky than all the old Urdu literature produced during the preceding two centuries.

In the present chapter an endeavour will be made to examine the outward form of this new literature and determine its indebtedness to English. For reasons explained in the Introduction, a chronological treatment of the subject will not be attempted. We shall therefore straightway proceed to notice what forms, undeniably English in structure, have either been newly incorporated into Urdu literature or have influenced those already in existence.

For the sake of clearness these forms may be classified into two convenient groups, either according to subject, under Poetry and Non-Poetry, or according to form, under Verse and Prose. As our immediate interest in this chapter is more in the form than in the substance or subject of Urdu literature, although a consideration of their inter-relation and even inter-dependence can hardly be avoided, it seems more appropriate to follow the latter division. In fact, inasmuch as Urdu poetry, with the possible exception of the new ouptut of dramatic writing, which is mainly in prose, and which orthodox literary opinion is so far reluctant to recognise as serious literature, is almost entirely in verse, the division according to form will practically resolve itself into a division according to substance. It will, moreover, present the subject of our discussion in proper historical perspective. For, as we have pointed out elsewhere, there was no prose in Urdu prior to the advent of English influence and all literature was exclusively in verse. The proposed division, therefore, will, by keeping the two separate, help us to trace the development of Urdu versification on the one hand, and to notice the rise and growth of Urdu prose on the other.

(ii) The Limitations of Early Versification

We shall take the department of verse first, which, as stated above, covers practically the whole of existing Urdu poetry. Before we enter upon an examination of this field, it will be helpful to suggest that as the practice of writing poetry in Urdu was long in existence and certain notions about poetic art had already found general acceptance in the country, the writers of the New School have found it rather hard to incorporate into Urdu poetry any new forms from English literature as freely as they have done in prose, where everything was new and where there was no fear of any clash with the ideals of any earlier literature. In fact the prosodic system borrowed from Persian, and through Persian from Arabic, indulged in such a large variety of metrical and stanzaic forms that any effort to load the list any further without any reference to the organic growth and genius of the language, and simply for the sake of imitation of the forms of a different literature, however great in itself, would have been a sheer waste of energy. It would have given even to the most sincere feeling, when expressed in unfamiliar forms, the touch of artificiality, a sin from which the leaders of the New Movement have been anxious to save their literature.

What we shall, therefore, find is not so much the incorporations of new forms from English prosody as the assimilation of the spirit underlying their formation.

It will be remembered that the great obstacle to freedom of expression lay in the technique of the different forms of Urdu poetry. For instance, in the *Ghazal* and the *Qaṣīda*, the most popular forms, it was a cardinal principle of Urdu prosody that every distich comprising it should end in the same rhyme. If the *Qaṣīda* happened to be, say, of ninety distichs, it followed that the composer should employ nearly the same number of words which would rhyme together. Some of the words might be repeated, but repetition took away from the merit of the composition. This insistence on the use of parallel rhyming words was the chief source of artificiality in early poetry. Too often it required the composer to select his words first, and then to think out ideas to suit these words. It was obviously a most unnatural order, and contributed greatly to the absence of continuity of thought and unity in the *Ghazal* and similar compositions. Owing to the existence in Arabic and Persian of a large number of words rhyming together which Urdu has always freely borrowed, some of the Urdu poets, such as Ghālib, occasionally succeeded in finding a group of words to suit their ideas, and thus introducing into a few of their *Ghazals and Qaṣīdas* a certain amount of unity. But that was more an exception than a rule.

Another source of artificiality in Urdu poetry was its conventional poetic diction, borrowed again from Persian and Arabic, the nature of which we have already, in a preceding chapter, tried to explain.

(iii) The Rise of the New School of Poetry

Sayyid Altāf Ḥusayn Ḥālī, the founder of the New School of Poetry in Urdu, was particularly struck by these outstanding defects in the poetry of his mother tongue. Born in 1837 [1] at Pānīpat, a few miles from Delhi, the home of Urdu poetry, he came at an early age under the influence of Mīrzā Asadu'llah Khān Ghālib of Delhi, probably the most original of the early Urdu poets. The age of Ghālib was still the age of convention, and neither the master nor the pupil could lightly dispense with the conventional style, although one might notice a certain amount of conscious attempt in the poems of Ghālib's maturer years and the early writings of Ḥālī to subordinate it to their thought and feeling. As the latter avowed,[2] he keenly felt the shackles of the stereotyped diction in his youth; but he had not the necessary boldness then, nor the force of example, nor any encouragement to break them and give the heart a loose rein.

This opportunity came to him in the middle of his life, when, owing to the vicissitudes which overtook respectable Muslim families of Delhi after the great Indian Mutiny in 1857, Ḥālī, like his contemporary and townsman, Muḥammad Ḥusayn Āzād, migrated from his home in search of employment and accepted service at Lahore in the educational department of the Government of the Punjab. Fortunately at the time this department was presided over by Col. W. R. N. Holroyd, whose name deserves to be remembered in connection with the development of Urdu poetry, as that of Dr. J. B. Gilchrist with the growth of Urdu prose. Under the sympathetic direction of this English officer, Ḥālī and Āzād were for some time engaged

[1] See obituary notice, *Institute Gazette Aligarh,* Jan. 6, 1915.
[2] See the Preface to *Musaddas-i-Ḥālī.*

in reviewing Urdu translations of standard English authors and also compiling suitable text-books in Urdu for use in Indian schools, fashioned no doubt on English models.[1] The personal contact with Col. Holroyd, together with what direct acquaintance they were able to form of some of the masterpieces of English literature in pursuance of their official duties, speedily stimulated their genius and awakened them to realise painfully by contrast that all was not well with their poetry, under whose spell they had so far wasted their powers, and that unless a new life was infused into it and its direction turned into fresh channels, there was a certain danger of its deteriorating still further, and seriously affecting the life of the rising generation.

The desire to improve their national poetry, which this awakening gave rise to, soon began to materialise. In 1874, at the instance of Āzād and Col. Holroyd, the Punjab Anjuman undertook to organise monthly " Mushā'iras " or meetings of poets where poems representing some of the features of English poetry were to be presented.[2] Of this organisation, the moving spirit was undoubtedly Āzād, although, realising his limitations as a poet, he did not contribute more than a few poems, of which the odes on the " Sunset," " Queen Victoria's Jubilee," and the *Kh̲wāb-i-Amn*, or " Slumber of Security," are still read with pleasure. Ḥālī's health did not permit him to stay in Lahore very long, and he could not attend more than four of these meetings, for every one of which, however, he wrote a poem. *Bārkha-rut* (Rainy Season) has the honour of being the first of this group, followed by *Nishāṭ-i-Umayd* (the Joy of Hope), *Ḥubb-i-Waṭan* (Love of Country), and *Munāẓara-i-Raḥm wa Inṣāf* (Dialogue between Mercy and Justice).

We shall discuss the form of these poems later on along

[1] See Preface to *Majmū'a-i-Naẓm-i-Ḥālī*, 1890, Delhi.

[2] *Ibid.* Also *Tahẕīb'l-Ak̲h̲lāq*, Faẓlu'd-Din's Collection, Vol. II., No. 635, Lahore, 1897.

with the others of *Ḥālī*. But it should be mentioned here that these four poems heralded the dawn of a new era in Urdu poetry. The year 1874 will thus be remembered as an epoch-making year in the history of Urdu literature, when the foundations of the New School of poetry were laid.

Recalling this "Mushā'ira" seventeen years after, and his first attempt under its auspices, Ḥālī observes :

"Had this movement taken its rise fifteen years earlier, it would probably not have borne any fruit. For such of those (literary men) in Hindustan as had any command over versification in Urdu (at the time) regarded poetry as synonymous with love-making, and exaggeration as an essential ingredient of poetic utterance, and imagined that the poetic rendering of facts and realities of life was contrary to the aims of true poetry. These men had never seen in their language any specimens of the literary art of the West on which they could have based their poetic effort. Fortunately, however, this movement took its rise at a time when the spirit of Western ideas was being infused into the Urdu language. A good many books and essays on literary subjects had already been translated from English, and many more were in the process of translation. In the native newspapers, of which the *Journal of the Scientific Society of Aligarh* desires special mention, translations of many articles from the English Press were being published. As a result, the style of Western writing was gradually gaining ground in the hearts of the people. So much so, that in 1872 Sir Sayyid Aḥmad Khān issued the Journal *Tahẕībᵘ-'l-Akhlāq* (Refining of Manners), through whose instrumentality there quickly came about a profound change in the ideas of those Muslims who had a right disposition for literature. Consequently the old style of Urdu and Persian writings began to appear in their eyes light and undignified. They began to look down with contempt on their system of poetry. There was then no good imitation of Western poetry in Urdu, nor has there been any till now. But sometimes even a little stir is enough: what little melody of Western literature had so far reached the seekers after new paths was enough to move them to enthusiasm. As a result, many a person whose mind was already deeply coloured by Eastern poetry began to take part in this 'Mushā'ira' (of 1874)." [1]

[1] See Preface to *Majmū'a-i-Naẕm-i-Ḥālī*, 1890, Delhi.

It will thus be seen that the new movement grew out of natural conditions and in response to the demands of those who were slowly imbibing the literary ideals of the West. This class of literary public was at first very limited in number. A large majority still adhered to the old ideals, although the observations of Ḥālī just quoted do not seem to take adequate cognisance of this fact. For the sake of a proper understanding of the situation when this movement was launched, it should be mentioned that the orthodox section far outnumbered those in favour of the new ideas, and though during the last fifty years the number of the former has gradually dwindled down, they still form at the present day a very important portion of the Muslim society of India. Ḥālī seems to have always been particularly anxious to keep this class in good humour. Whenever he published any poems or wrote any articles on any literary subject, he was always full of apology for anything he said which he felt would not easily commend itself to them. In fact, in the preface to the collection of his poems published in 1892, from which the extract quoted above is taken, he makes the following rather strange confession of his ignorance of the literary ideals of the West, which, as those who have read his masterly Prologomena to his *Dīwān*, which appeared about the same time, will at once recognise, is a large concession to his orthodox critics. He says :

"Neither had I any acquaintance, then (1874), with the principles of Western poetry, nor have I now (1890). Indeed, in my opinion, a satisfactory imitation of Western poetry is not possible in an undeveloped language like Urdu. No doubt, to a certain extent, I had by disposition a natural aversion to exaggeration and immoderate language. To a certain extent this aversion was deepened by the new movement; excepting that, there is nothing in my writings which can be cited as an imitation of English poetry or as a revolt against the old style of writing." [1]

[1] See Preface to *Majmū'a-i-Naẓm-i-Ḥālī*, 1890, Delhi.

We shall revert to this attitude of Ḥālī when we come to discuss the spirit and content of his writings. At this place we shall merely emphasise what we have stated before, that the new movement in Urdu poetry took its rise in Lahore not a moment too soon, and that Ḥālī, in spite of his modesty was the most important and the best exponent of it.

On leaving Lahore, Ḥālī came under the influence of (Sir) Sayyid Aḥmad, whose inspiring personality, and the ideals of the Aligarh movement which he led, profoundly affected the mind of Ḥālī, as is borne out by the high tone and purpose of the poems he wrote during the rest of his life, especially of his *Flow and Ebb of Islam*, 1879, *Complaint of India*, 1887, *The Education of Muslims*, 1889, and *The Widow's Plaint*, 1892.

(iv) New Spirit in Old Forms

What then was the nature of this influence on the mind and art of Ḥālī as manifested in the form of his writings ?

As suggested at the beginning of this section, Ḥālī did not feel called upon to borrow any new stanzaic forms from English poetry. He was rightly of opinion that the Urdu language was not sufficiently developed at the time to lend itself either to blank verse or to any of the typical English stanzaic arrangements. Any premature attempts would not only have been attended by failure, but would have brought the new movement into disrepute. He, however, turned his attention to introducing into his poems, as far as the language allowed, two of the chief elements which characterised English writings, viz., *unity of idea*, which implied an unimpeded flow and freedom in expression, and a *diction free from convention*—elements which were absent from Urdu poetry of the preceding centuries. The former was not hitherto possible because of the conditions of rhyme in the most popular forms; the latter was not thought of because of the wrong tastes formed by the example of Persian poetry.

The work before Ḥālī was therefore quite clear, difficult though it undoubtedly was of achievement. It was on the one hand to keep rhyme under proper control so as not to let it interfere with the freedom of thought and expression, and on the other to dispense with the conventional diction altogether.

It will be remembered that of all the forms in Urdu poetry the *G͟hazal* and *Qaṣīda* devote the greatest amount of attention to rhyme. Ḥālī felt called upon to avoid them. Not that he did not express himself in these forms in his later years. He did, especially in the former. But that was on very rare occasions, and solely with a view to complete his *Dīwān*, which was nothing more than satisfying a technical requirement. None of his principal writings, on which his reputation as a poet of the New School rests, is in either of these artificial forms.

Ḥālī's studied indifference to *G͟hazal* and *Qaṣīda* against the prevalent taste was a great step forward. It was one brave attempt to free himself from the restrictions which had clogged the freedom of expression and introduced the element of artificiality not only in the works of his predecessors but his own early writings. It led him to search for other forms from the existing list such as in his opinion did not impede the flow of thought and feeling to the same extent as the *G͟hazal* and *Qaṣīda* did.

Of the forms which he largely employed for this purpose, *Musaddas* and *Maṣnawī* deserve special mention. As described elsewhere, the former is a stanza of six lines consisting of a quatrain followed by a rhymed couplet; and the latter is the Arabic term for the rhymed couplet, in none of which is the poet required to employ more than two to four words rhyming together. If we exclude blank verse out of consideration, it may without exaggeration be asserted that *Musaddas* and the *Maṣnawī* afford the writer as much freedom as any form in English literature.

Musaddas.—His greatest work, *The Flow and Ebb of Islam*, is in the *Musaddas*. It is the longest poem ever attempted in that form in the Urdu language. The greatness of the theme of the poem and the beauty of its diction has popularised the form to such an extent that the work is generally known not so much by its name as by the stanzaic form in which it is written. It is called *Musaddas-i-Ḥālī*, or the *Musaddas* of Ḥālī. An important feature of this form is the ease with which it lends itself to the expression of the elegaic or reflective mood. The feeling rises to a climax at the end of the fourth line, subsiding in the last two. On a smaller scale its structure, representing this rise and fall in feeling, may be said to correspond to that of the sonnet, though the similarity is not on all fours with any one of its two well-known types. The rise is more like the rise in the octave opening the Petrarchan and the fall like that in the rhymed couplet closing the Shakespearean sonnet. The rise and fall are thus not proportionately distributed. The rise in the *Musaddas* being gradual and within bounds, needed a gradual fall as in the Petrarchan sestett, and not so abrupt as in the Shakespearean form, where it is apparently justified by the long and sustained character of the rise, which out of sheer exhaustion speedily loses itself in the rhymed couplet. Because of this artistic incompleteness there is not a sense of finality in the mind of the reader at the end of each *Musaddas*. There is always the feeling that something is to follow, that each fall is calling for and looking forward to a rise. It is like a wave rushing at a steep shore and quickly receding, only to be lost or pushed back again by the next following close behind it.

Ḥālī seems to have fully realised the value of such a stanza. It gave him on the one hand adequate freedom from the restrictions of rhyme, and on the other, by virtue of its structural peculiarity of letting one stanza anticipate another, a powerful aid and motive power to the development and expansion of his theme. The success with which he has handled this form in his *Flow aad Ebb of Islam* is a great landmark in the history of Urdu versification. Since its publication in 1879, every aspirant to the distinction of poet—and the number is legion, for, owing to the prevailing tendency, everyone capable of manipulating a few words rhyming together very usually assumes a *Takhalluṣ*, or poetical surname, and feels entitled to write poetry—has invariably felt inclined to try his hand at *Musaddas.* Even a writer like Ḥāfiz Naẕīr Aḥmad, whose genius was moulded entirely for prose, could not escape the temptation. So large and varied has been the output, during recent years, of so-called poetic literature in *Musaddas*, in imitation of the style of Ḥālī, that it is hardly possible, in a survey such as this, to deal with it at any length. Excepting a very small portion, all of it has already sunk into oblivion. Much of it originally appeared in the flimsy sheets of the Urdu daily newspaper, and has consequently shared the inevitable fate of such publications. Of the few poems which have managed to survive so far may be mentioned the *Shikwa* (Complaint) and *Jawāb-i-Shikwa* (Reply to Complaint) of Dr. Sir Muḥammad Iqbāl of Lahore.

Maṣnawī is another important form which Ḥālī chose to employ in order to facilitate freedom of thought and expression in his poetic utterance. As stated above, it is a distich after the style of the heroic couplet of Pope and Dryden. It lends itself to several metrical variations usually ranging from six to ten syllables in each line, and for that reason possesses a flexibility such as is not possible in the heroic couplet—a flexibility which renders *Maṣnawī* such a convenient and valuable vehicle of expression of every mood. It is a form which is particularly suited for narrative and descriptive poetry. *Bīwa kī Munājāt* (Widow's Plaint), *Ḥubb-i-Waṭan* (Love of Country), and *Bārkha-rut* (Rainy

Season) of Ḥālī, the *Shām ki Āmad awr Rāt kī Kayfiyyat* (Advent of Evening and the Scene of Night) of Muḥammad Ḥusayn Āzād, and the *Ṣubḥ-i-Umayd* (Dawn of Hope) of Shiblī are probably the best of the *Maṣnawīs* attempted by the writers of the New School. In the polish and sweetness of the language, these new *Maṣnawīs* may not quite excel the older *Maṣnawīs* of *Badr-i-Munīr* and *Gulzār-i-Nasīm*, but, in execution of their respective themes, they certainly are a great advance on them. The subject is always steadily kept in view. The digressions are subordinated to the central interest. Exaggeration, superfluities and meaningless sentimentality and peroration are studiously avoided. The attempt is to say a thing in a simple, clear, straightforward style, and to say it in such a way as to give the reader a unified effect.

Other forms.—Three other forms—*Rubā'ī* (quatrain), *Maqṭ'a* (Fragment), and the *Tarkīb-Band* (Composite Tie)—have also found favour with the writers of the New School.

The *Rubā'ī* is probably the most difficult of compositions. It is usually employed to give expression to some deep conviction or observation on one or other of the problems of human life. As each *Rubā'ī* is complete in itself, the task of the composer to bring out a great idea in but four lines is by no means easy. It argues on his part the sense of right perspective, a wide experience of men and things and a talent for brevity of expression. The *Rubā'ī* is thus usually the prerogative of a mature mind, and none but the ablest has been found to handle it successfully. Of all the poets and poetasters of modern times, only Mīr Anīs of Lucknow, Ḥālī and Muḥammad Akbar Ḥusayn of Allahabad have been able to give us some of the best *Rubā'īyyāt* ever composed in the Urdu language.

Maqt'a (Fragment) is another form which calls for restraint and sobriety of expression such as only may be expected of well-cultivated minds. For that reason there are but few writers who have found it convenient to attempt anything in this form. Hālī has written some very good *Maqt'as*, but they are probably not so nearly perfect as some of those attempted by his contemporary, Shiblī. In fact the "Fragment" has been the most favourite form with the latter. His poems entitled *An Incident of the Reign of Fārūq* (Caliph 'Umar), *A Supreme Example of Self-Sacrifice, The Real Cause of the Decadence of Islam,* and his *Address to the Viceroy* (Lord Hardinge of Penshurst), are some of the best specimens which the Urdu language possesses of this form of poetry.

Tarkīb-Band is one more form which has appealed to the writers of the New School. *The Complaint of India* of Ḥālī is by far the best of the Urdu poems ever written in this form.

By employing these several forms and avoiding subjects which require the use of conventional diction, the writers of the New School have to a great extent succeeded in introducing into their poetic writings a measure of that freedom of thought and feeling and expression so characteristic of English literature. The success which has been achieved so far would not have been possible had the writers attempted to express themselves through absolutely unfamiliar forms. No doubt there were some amateurish attempts to imitate the blank verse and a few of the stanzaic arrangements of English poets—attempts which by their obvious strangeness hardly found favour with the general public.

(v) Wholly New Forms from English

Some of these may be mentioned here. In the issue of May 1899 of the now defunct *Dilgudāz*, there appeared a translation of Gray's "Elegy Written in a Country Churchyard," by Mawlawī Sayyid 'Alī Ḥaydar *Ṭabāṭabāī'* (now Nawwāb Ḥaydar Yār Jang), sometime Professor of Arabic,

Nizam College, Hyderabad, Deccan. The aim of the translator was evidently to effect a literal rendering of the poem in as many lines and stanzas as there were in the original, and observing the same rhyme order throughout, viz. *a b a b*. A similar attempt was made a month after by one Mr. Sayyid Muḥammad Ẓāmin, who translated the verses entitled "A Ballad" in Goldsmith's *Vicar of Wakefield.*

'Abd^u'l-Ḥalīm Sharar, whose work as the leading novelist of the period under review will come up for consideration later on, has given us an incomplete dramatic play in *blank verse,* dealing with an incident of the time of the downfall of the Arab power in Spain. The play was intended to appear by instalments in the *Dilgudāz,* of which Sharar was the editor. The first instalment, consisting of the first scene of the opening act, was published in June 1900, with an introductory note by the author to the effect that the subsequent instalments would soon follow if the public extended to him the necessary indulgence. In September came the second instalment of one more scene, with an editorial note expressing gratification at the encouraging welcome accorded to the previous contribution by some unnamed friends of the author. In the following month was given the third scene, but without any comments whatsoever. And then was heard no more of the play. Why the attempt was given up is all a matter of conjecture. Possibly the enthusiasm of the author's friends was not strong enough to last long, or the author himself realised the futility of his venture.

'Abd^u'l-Halīm Sharar is unquestionably one of the most outstanding figures in Urdu prose. Success in one department seems to have raised in him hopes of success in every other. He therefore applied his hand to poetry and versification. Had he employed any of the indigenous forms, he might very likely have been able to know whether his attempts were worth publication. But when he ventured to write a piece of drama in blank verse in imitation of Shakespeare and at the same time hoped, as he expressed in the introductory note, that he might thereby "lay the foundation of blank verse in Urdu language," he seems to have hardly realised that he was undertaking much too great a task for him. Blank verse is not made by just drawing a dividing line at the end of each tenth syllable, or at the end of every fourteenth, as he seems to have done. There is no doubt that Sharar knew this perfectly well. But his production hardly indicates this. In fact, in his natural desire to write in a style different from prose, he has given us something which is neither prose nor verse.

A couple of months after Sharar had laid down his pen, Nawwāb Ḥaydar Yār Jang Tabāṭabāī', translator of Gray's *Elegy*, felt inclined to take up the forlorn cause of blank verse, in Urdu. Luckily he did not aim so high as Sharar nor set out to write a piece of drama in the style of Shakespeare. In fact he had no pretensions in that direction. Being, however, a great lover of Urdu, and a great believer in its capacity for expression, he seems to have felt keenly the apparent failure which attended the effort of Sharar, who appears to have once been his pupil,[1] and thereby thought of handling the blank verse himself with a view, no doubt, to show to the public that a successful attempt was not beyond the bounds of possibility in Urdu language. He did not, as Sharar did, look back into the distant and romantic past of Muslim Spain for a suitable poetic theme for treatment in blank verse. He chose the subject of "blank verse" itself for rendering in blank verse! As a staunch adherent of the orthodox canons of prosody in Urdu, he could not call blank verse, verse properly so called, for there was no place for rhyme in it. So, while Sharar

[1] See Sharar's editorial note to Ṭabāṭabāī''s contribution, *Dilgudāz*, 1900.

was catholic enough to translate "blank verse" in Urdu as *Naẓm-i-G͟hayr-Muqaffa*, or "verse without rhyme," Ṭabāṭabāī' translated it as *Naṣr-i-Murajjaz*, or "measured or rhythmic prose," which was a recognised form in Urdu writing. He therefore entitled his contribution "Blank Verse or Measured Prose in the Metre of Quatrain." It is evidently a very interesting title. "Blank verse" may not seem such an attractive subject for poetic treatment. Still there is no reason why one should not choose it. More prosaic subjects have sometimes excited the finest poetic thoughts. There could, therefore, be no quarrel with Ṭabāṭabāī' on that score. Nor need one grumble at his somewhat pedantic fastidiousness in preferring the expression "measured prose" to "verse without rhyme." It does not make any material difference so long as one understands clearly that both expressions were but genuine attempts to express the same idea connoted by English "blank verse." What, however, is difficult of comprehension in the title of Ṭabāṭabāī''s contribution is the principle underlying the suggested *liaison* between blank verse as understood in English and the quatrain on the one hand, and *Nasr-i-Murajjaz*, or rhythmic prose as recognised in Urdu and the metre of *Rubā'ī* or quatrain, on the other. According to English rules of prosody, blank verse needs to be always expressed in iambic pentameter. It may be possible to write unrhymed verse in English in any other metre, but such a verse will not be entitled to the name of "blank verse." To think of writing blank verse in any but iambic pentameter and to divide it into stanzas of four lines each as Ṭabāṭabāī' has done, is, to say the least of it, not warranted by English example, which he evidently set out to imitate. Division of blank verse into stanzas will defeat the very purpose for which it has been primarily designed, viz. to give poetic thought and feeling the fullest freedom of expression. Nor, do we think, is there any precedent in Urdu literature, or allowance in Urdu prosody, for cutting out *Naṣr-i-Murajjaz* into lines of ten to fourteen syllables and arbitrarily arranging them in groups of four lines each. It would certainly be a different thing if Ṭabāṭabāī' had presented his stanza as a new invention altogether, for then we could have examined it on its own intrinsic merits; but when he has attempted to get it accepted under old names and for what it is not, we feel reluctant to observe that he has set his expectations rather too high. Here is a literal translation of the opening stanza of his *Blank Verse or Measured Prose in the Metre of Quatrain.*

(1) "There are three recognised forms of prose. Of these
(2) Measured prose is one; that is, that expression
(3) In which there is poetic metre and in which rhyme
(4) Restriction is non-existing; Idea should be free."[1]

Whether such a piece of composition should be entitled to recognition as literature will not be very difficult to decide. To us it seems that an orthodox poet of the standing of Tabātabāī', and a purist in style such as he, should never have lent his pen to writing of this description.

Another attempt at imitation of English forms deserving of notice is by one Muḥammad Azhar 'Alī Āzād Kakūrī, sometime Deputy Taḥṣīldār in the District of Gorakhpur, a writer not much known to the literary public. In the Oriental Section of the Library of the British Museum there is an undated copy of a play by him in rhymed verse entitled, "*Jām-i-Ulfat* (Goblet of Affection), or the translation of Shakespeare's well-known drama of *A Midsummer Night's Dream,*" printed at the "Ryāẓu'l-Akhbār Press," Gorakhpur. The title is misleading, for the play is not a translation but merely an adaptation. What, however, interests us here is his attempt to imitate the metrical language used by Puck and the fairies in the Shakespeare original.

[1] Special translation.

Referring to this in his introduction to the play, the writer has given expression to some interesting observations which may be reproduced here. Says he :

"The fairies of Shakespeare are in stature just of the size of a thumb. It would, therefore, be too incongruous to endow them with tongues of the length of a hand. Indeed it is a matter for consideration whether it would be possible for people of such diminutive dimensions to speak in metrical lines each a yard in length. It seems proper that the lines which emanate from their mouths should be as small as their size. The author (Shakespeare) has observed this condition in the original. Unfortunately, however, there is no such short metre in our language. Still, after some consideration, I thought out a device by which I could safely follow the example—and that was to employ tiny verses as warranted under the circumstances, in such a manner that every four of them should make a hemistich, and every eight a rhymed couplet so as to fulfil the conditions of Urdu prosody, as follows :

Kahīn Ṣaḥn-i-Chaman,
Kahīn Bāgh-i-'Adan,
Kahīn Barg-i-Saman,
Kahīn Āb-i-Rawān. } *First hemistich.*

Kabhī Lāl-i-Yaman,
Kabhī Mushk-i-Khutan,
Kabhī Yih Gulshan,
Kabhī wah Bustun." } *Second hemistich.*[1]

Barring these few spasmodic and apparently inadequate attempts, very little has been done to incorporate into the system of Urdu prosody any new forms from English versification. The primary concern of the leading poets has been, as already explained, to get rid of the most pressing shackles of convention, and introduce elements of simplicity, clearness and naturalness into poetic utterance. The amount of success which has attended their efforts may not be what one would have desired, but it is enough to dispel every doubt as to further possibilities. It would,

[1] Special translation.

no doubt, be invidious to compare an infant poetic literature like modern Urdu, with one so vast in scope and extent and so great in quality as English. But in order to have an idea of the degree of improvement effected in the form and diction of Urdu poetry during the last half-century, it may be stated without exaggeration that the new literary movement has produced a few poems such as the *Flow and Ebb of Islam*, *Love of Country*, *Widow's Plaint*, *Complaint of India*, and *Invocation to the Prophet*, which, in simplicity and naturalness of diction, and depth and flow of thought and feeling and even imagination, may be worthily placed side by side with any English poems treating of *similar subjects*, and expressed in *rhymed verse*.

(vi) Results Analysed

Before we close this part of our subject it is but fair to acknowledge that the credit for this striking development rests essentially with the late Ḥālī. Others, no doubt, there have been, especially the late Akbar of Allahabad and the late Shiblī, who have contributed their own share to it. But Ḥālī stands above them all, the leader and inspirer of the movement, who has set the fashion for the rest, whose contribution exceeds in bulk that of any other, and whose writings represent some of the salient features of English poetry to a degree hardly attained by any among his contemporaries or even among the present generation of poets, the best known of whom is Dr. Sir Muḥammad Iqbāl of Lahore. This latter group, mostly the product of modern English education, are the exponents of that sentimental or emotional idealism which has taken its rise among a certain section of the Indian Muslim community, in the wàke of the vicissitudes which have overtaken the Turkish Empire during the last fifteen years. We shall in a subsequent chapter speak at some length of their contribution to poetic thought in Urdu literature. But in this place, concerned as we are with its outward form and technique, it should be pointed out that the present-day writers have not, so far, made any advance on what was effected by Ḥālī and his contemporaries. In fact, if we accept the writings of Dr. Iqbāl as the best specimen of the literary productions of this latest school of sentimental poetry, we shall not fail to notice a distinct retrogression, a return to the style of the poets whom Ḥālī had deliberately relegated to the limbo of oblivion. This aspect will at once force itself on our attention when we place the *Flow and Ebb of Islam* of Hālī, and the *Complaint* and *Reply to the Complaint* of Iqbāl side by side—both treating of the same subject and both written in the same stanza. In the one there is simplicity, clearness, grace and beauty of language and diction and a marvellous control over the form and subject. Above all there is an utter disregard of convention. In the other there is no doubt a certain charm of expression suggestive of deep feeling, but none of the outstanding qualities characterising the *Flow and Ebb of Islam*. Iqbāl's *Complaint* begins in the conventional style, and in the conventional language. The conventional touch is present throughout. Words and phrases and figures of speech which for centuries have formed the stock-in-trade of the composer of the love and Ṣūfistic songs are freely employed. There is too much artifice in expression and very little simplicity. It might be urged that the theme of the poem, being so grand, called for a grand style. But a grand style is not synonymous with pomposity. Nor is it opposed to clearness. Any poem or any piece of literature which fails to produce an unified effect is defective to that extent. The *Complaint* is a collection of sentiments such as will excite the vanity or pride of the Indian Muslims, each of which may be pleasing in itself but which together hardly convey any definite or clear idea.

In another place we will discuss these sentiments, such as they are, in order to appraise the nature of Iqbāl's poetic thought in relation to that of other poets. But here we cannot refrain from observing that his art does not by any means reach the standard and excellence of that of Ḥālī; and in fact does not show any clear traces of the influence of the forms and technique of English poetry such as the other does.

While Urdu prose has been making remarkable progress in almost every direction, Urdu verse remains where it was left by Ḥālī and his contemporaries.

CHAPTER VI

NEW FORMS AND TECHNIQUE—PROSE

(i) No Prose in Urdu before English Influence

Passing from verse to prose, we enter upon an absolutely new field, a field which, if we may so express it, was discovered, cleared of the undergrowth, ploughed and harrowed, and prepared for cultivation by English agencies, and on which we now see a luxuriant growth of various crops sprung from seeds which must have originally belonged to an entirely different clime.

As we have pointed out in a preceding chapter, there was from the time of Amīr Khusraw (fifteenth century), one of the first to attempt verse in Urdu language, down to the close of the eighteenth century, no prose whatsoever in Urdu. One generation of poets after another arose and disappeared, having done what they could to purify and polish the rustic jargon of the city of Delhi and increase its capacity for literary expression. Few ever thought of employing it for purposes of prose. From the simplest business letter to the most elaborate composition in history or philosophy or religion, everything was attempted in Persian. Even prefaces to poetic works in Urdu were written in Persian.

With Persian playing such an important rôle, it is no wonder that literary men felt little inclination to evolve prose in Urdu. One or two attempts have, however, come down to us from the first half of the eighteenth century. The poet Faẓlī, who flourished in the reign of Emperor Muḥammad Shāh, is reputed to be the author of a religious poem, *Dah Majlis*, to which is prefixed an introductory note in Urdu prose. Muḥammad Ḥusayn Āzād is of opinion that it is probably the earliest contribution to Urdu prose. Mīrza Rafī[su]'s-Sawdā is another poet who made a similar attempt. A few sentences are also attributed to the poet Sayyid Inshā' and Mīrzā Jān-i-Jānān.[1]

Beyond these few instances, nothing seems to have been done in this direction. From the nature of the compositions, one will at once notice that they are but amateurish attempts expressed in a heavy and cumbersome style and written in a language hardly distinguishable from the Indo-Persian in vogue in the later days of the Mogul Empire.

We may therefore for all practical purposes safely assume that there was no prose in Urdu down to the close of the eighteenth century—nothing, at all events, in the form of literature.

(ii) Rise of Prose under English Influence

Strange as it might appear, the first serious effort to lay the foundation of Urdu prose was made by a Scotsman, John Borthwick Gilchrist.[2] Born in 1759 at Edinburgh, educated at George Heriot's Hospital in that city, he went out to Calcutta in 1883 as Medical Officer in the service of the East India Company. At this time the policy of the Company was to acquaint its employees with a working knowledge of Persian, which was the language of the courts and the Government. From his personal experience it, however, appeared to Gilchrist that this policy was at variance with the best interests of the British official class.[3] For Persian was not the language of the people, and on that account no helpful and direct intercourse was possible through its medium. He was therefore of opinion that so

[1] See *Āb-i-Ḥayāt*; also *Gulshan-i-Hind.*

[2] For an account of his life and work see the following: Memoir in Chambers' *Eminent Scotsmen*, ii. 106–7; *Annual Register*, 1841, lxxxiii. 181; *East India Register*, 1803, Part I, 83; W. Anderson's *Scottish Nation*, ii. 298–300; *Dictionary of National Biography.*

[3] Similar views were held by a few other English residents in India. See *Calcutta Review*, 1845.

long as the British officers neglected to study the vernaculars of the country, particularly Hindustani or Urdu, the common and the most prevalent form of speech, they could not hope rightly to enter into the needs and aspirations of the people under their charge and secure a hold on their affection. He himself came forward to set the example.

"Clad in native garb, he travelled through those provinces where Hindustani was spoken in its greatest purity, and also acquired good knowledge of Sanskrit, Persian and other Eastern languages. His success inspired a new spirit in the Company's servants, and the study of Hindustani became most popular."

In order to help the study of this language, Gilchrist published *A Dictionary, English and Hindustani*, in two parts, in 1796, followed by the *Oriental Linguist, an Introduction to the Language of Hindustani*, in 1798.[1]

Lord Wellesley, who was appointed to the Governor-Generalship of India in 1798, was not slow in recognising the importance of the work which Gilchrist had voluntarily imposed upon himself. He not only liberally aided him from the Company's revenues, but appointed him head of the Fort William College founded in 1800 to instruct British servants of the Company in the languages of the country. Gilchrist could not, however, long enjoy this position. Owing to ill-health, he was allowed to retire in 1804 on a pension of £300.

Although he was thus unfortunately cut off from the field of his favourite work, he did not lose his interest in it on his retirement. After staying in Edinburgh till 1816, he "removed to London and undertook private tuition in Oriental languages to candidates for Indian services," and in 1818 accepted the Professorship of Hindustani at the Oriental Institute, Leicester Square, established

[1] For an account of earlier attempts made in this field by European scholars see Grierson: *A Bibliography of Western Hindi including Hindustani.*

in that year by the East India Company for the benefit especially of medical officers proceeding to India. Owing to differences which arose between him and the authorities of the Company, the Institute was abolished in 1825, and with it his Chair of Hindustani. He, however, continued to hold his classes privately for nearly a year, when he handed them over to the Orientalists, Sandford Arnot and Duncan Forbes. Thereafter his life was rather uneventful. He died at the age of eighty-two in Paris on the 9th of January, 1841.

For the purpose of our subject we are specially concerned with his work between 1796, when he first published his Dictionary at Calcutta, till 1804, when he handed over the charge of his Principalship of the Fort William College and returned to Scotland.

During these nine years, both in his private pursuit of knowledge and his capacity as the official head of the Fort William College, he was interested in the compilation of suitable text-books for the use of British officials desirous of making a study of Urdu. In the course of his wide travels among Urdu-speaking people, he had come across a great many scholars, and had marked out a few among them as worthy of enlistment in his cause. So when he was called upon to direct the affairs of the Fort William College, Gilchrist lost no time in inviting their co-operation. Of those who responded to his call must be mentioned Sher 'Alī Afsūs, Sayyid Muḥammad Ḥaydar Bakhsh Ḥaydarī, Mīr Amman, Mīr Bahādur 'Alī Ḥusaynī, Hafīẓu'd-Dīn Aḥmad, and Mīrza 'Alī Luṭf.

It should be remembered that none of these literary men had ever applied their hand to prose. But they were masters of Urdu idiom, and Dr. Gilchrist felt from his personal acquaintance with them that under proper guidance they would succeed in writing readable prose. To have asked them to attempt original work would have meant time, and Dr. Gilchrist seemed in no particular mood to wait. He was anxious to have suitable text-books as quickly as possible. Translation was the only other alternative. He would obviously have been pleased to have placed in their hands standard works from English for such a purpose. But few of them at first knew even the rudiments of English. He had therefore perforce to let the writers undertake the translation of such popular books from Persian as in his view would lend themselves easily to a clear and simple style in translation which would appeal to English students.

It will thus be seen that the work before the translators was to introduce, in however small a measure, into the Urdu translations, some of the elements of English prose writing, such as naturalness of expression, clearness, simplicity and avoidance of conceits.

That the writers succeeded beyond the wildest expectations of Dr. Gilchrist is amply borne out by the fact that although marvellous improvement has been effected in the style of Urdu prose since their time, their productions are still held in popular esteem and not only are widely read by the common people, but are still, in some provinces, used as text-books for Indian schools. At the present day it may not be quite possible to agree with the *Encyclopædia Britannica* that they "are still *unsurpassed* as specimens of elegant and serviceable prose composition" (Ninth Edition, xi. 849), but no one, it is hoped, will ever venture to deny that they have contributed in no small measure to the very high standard of prose which Urdu writers have attained during recent years.

It may seem idle to surmise as to what turn Urdu prose would have taken if it had developed under different auspices; but the present writer cannot help feeling that what has happened has happened for the best. Had Amīr Khusraw or even Walī and their contemporaries cared to evolve prose as they did Urdu verse, and passed it on to the successors such as they had, it might possibly have become gradually as wooden and artificial as the other had when Ḥālī came forward fifty years ago to arrest its further declension. Fortunately, however, it came into existence at the suggestion and to meet the needs of the representatives of a people who had themselves a rich, noble and flourishing literature of their own, and who were consequently entitled to nourish the child of their creation on wholesome means of sustenance and give it a proper start in life. That seems to be the reason why Urdu prose has so speedily developed into such a powerful factor in the present literary renaissance of the Muslim community of India. The progress which it has made since Gilchrist left the shores of India may in some measure be comprehended when it is suggested that, but for the difference of language, writers such as Shiblī, Ḥālī, Āzād, Sir Sayyid Aḥmad, Nawwab Muḥsinu'l-Mulk, and 'Abd[u]'l-Ḥalīm Sharar might worthily have secured a recognised position as masters of style in English literature. So great and far-reaching has been the effect of the lead given by the late Dr. Gilchrist to the translators employed by the East India Company in the time of Lord Wellesley!

As these writings are thus a landmark in the history of Urdu prose literature, it seems desirable to mention the most important of them.

Sher 'Alī Afsūs.—His writings include *Bāgh-i-Urdū* (1799),[1] being the translation of the famous *Gulistān* or "Rose Garden" of Shaykh S'adī of Persia, and *Ārā'ish-i-Maḥfil* or Ornament of Assembly (1805),[2] a short history of the Hindu kings of Delhi from Judhister to Rai Pithoura, compiled primarily from *Khulāṣat[u]'t-Tawārīkh*, a Persian

[1] Translated into English by H. M. Court, pp. xviii, 354, Allahabad, 1871, 8vo., and revised and corrected, pp. vi, 198, Calcutta, 1882, 8vo.

[2] Translated into English by N. E. Benmobel, pp. xviii, 49, Dublin, 1847, 8vo. One of the editions published with an English preface by W. Nassau Lees, pp. viii, 300, Calcutta, 1863, 8vo.

work by Sajan Rāi of Patiala. He also revised in 1804 *Maẕhab-i-'Ishq* (Religion of Love), generally known as *Gul-i-Bakāwalī*, a translation undertaken under the superintendence of Dr. Gilchrist by Munshī Nihāl Chand from the original in Persian by Izzatu'llah Bangāli. It is an imaginary story of a man, Taju'l-Mulūk, falling in love with a fairy by name Bakāwalī.

Sayyid Muḥammad Ḥaydur Bakhsh Ḥaydarī.—He wrote the *Ṭuṭā Kahānī*[1] (Parrot Story) in 1801, based on the *Ṭuṭī-nāmā* of Ibn Nishātī, who flourished at the Court of Quṭb 'Alī Shāh of Bījāpūr. He also translated the celebrated Persian tale *Qiṣṣa-i-Ḥātim Ṭā'ī*, and also *Bahār-i-Dānish*, and compiled short biographical accounts of the early martyrs of Islam under the title of *Gul-i-Maghfirat*,[2] or Flower of Redemption. He is also known to have translated some Persian account of the invasion of Nādir Shāh and the sack of Delhi in 1839.

Mīr Amman.—He rendered into Urdu prose the famous tale of the Four Dervishes, otherwise known as *Bāgh-o-Bahār*,[3] originally written in Persian by Amīr Khusraw. This is probably the most important work executed under the direction of Dr. Gilchrist. It is written in a very simple and pleasing style, and was for some time popular with the Urdu-knowing section of the Anglo-Indian population in India.

Mīr Bahādur 'Alī Ḥusaynī.—He rendered into Urdu prose the celebrated Urdu Masnawī *Siḥr^{u}'l-Bayān*, or the love story of Badr-i-Munīr and Bī-Naẓīr of *Mīr Ḥasan.* Two more works written in 1812 in prose are attributed to him. One is *Akhlāq-i-Hindī*, or Indian Ethics, based on an earlier Persian work, *Mufarriḥ^{u}'l-Qulūb* of Muftī Tāj^{u}'d-Dīn, which

[1] Translated into English, 1875.

[2] Translated into French by M. Garcin de Tassy, pp. vii, 342. Paris, 1845, 8vo.

[3] There are various translations of this in English and French.

again is a version of the Sanskrit *Hitopadesa*, or Salutary Counsel. The other is *Ta'rīkh-i-Āshām*, being an account of the expedition into Assam of Mīr Jumla, the famous general of Emperor Awrangzayb in the year 1662. It was compiled from the Persian work of the same name by Shihābu'd-Dīn Tālish.

Hafīẓu'd-Dīn Aḥmad.—He translated, under the name of Khirad Afrūz (Illuminating the Intellect or Understanding), the well-known work *'Iyār-i-Dānish* of Abu'l-Faẓl ibn Mubārak, a Persian version of Bīdpāi's Book of Fables, founded on Ḥusayn ibn 'Alī al-Kāshifī's Persian work *Anwār-i-Suhaylī*.

Mīrza 'Alī Luṭf.—There is only one known work by this writer, entitled *Gulshan-i-Hind* (Garden of Hind), written in 1801. It is a *tazkira* or collection of short biographical sketches of Urdu poets from the earliest times down to the close of the eighteenth century, based on the Persian *Gulzār-i-Hind* of 'Alī Ibr'ahīm Khān of Lucknow.[1]

These writings, which together assume considerable bulk, and which one and all were undertaken under the immediate supervision of Dr. Gilchrist, will assuredly hand down

[1] It is interesting to note that a copy of it presumed to have belonged to one of the private libraries washed away in one of the Musi floods of Hyderabad, Deccan, was, it is said, quite by accident picked up from the debris, and brought to the notice of Mr. Ghulām Muḥammad, an Assistant Secretary to the Nizam's Government, who passed it on to the Librarian of the Āsifiyya State Library. It was subsequently revised and edited with notes by the late Shiblī, and published at Lahore in 1906 with an introduction by Mr. 'Abdu'l-Ḥaq, Secretary of the "Anjuman-i-Taraqqī-i-Urdū."

In his introduction, Mr. 'Abdu'l-Ḥaq says that had it not been for the recovery of this unique copy, *Gulshan-i-Hind* would have been absolutely lost to literature. Was it the only copy of the book ever written? M. Garcin de Tassy used some copy of *Gulshan-i-Hind* when he compiled in 1839 his *Histoire de la Littérature et Hindostani.* Mawlawi Karīmu'd-Din and Mr. F. Fallon speak of having consulted another copy in connection with their work *Ṭabaqāt-i-Shu'arā-i-Hind,* published at the Delhi College in 1848.

his name to posterity. Their permanent value lies in having laid the foundation of Urdu prose and given a tone —an English tone—to subsequent attempts in that field of literature.

Urdu prose has since progressed at a remarkably rapid pace. The rise of the printing press in the country, the activities of translating agencies such as the Scientific Societies of Delhi and Aligarh, the "Dā,iratᵘ'l-Ma'ārif" and the Osmania University of Hyderabad, Deccan, the All-India Muhammadan Educational Conference and its auxiliary bodies, the "Anjuman-i-Taraqqi-i-Urdu," the Christian Bible and Tract Societies, and a host of minor associations all over the country, have during the last hundred years, particularly since the Mutiny in 1857, vastly increased the capacity of the language as a vehicle of literary and scientific expression by incorporating, sometimes bodily, sometimes with modifications, a large number of English words and idioms, modes of expresssion, and literary and scientific terminology, and thus produced a great body of literature in prose fashioned distinctly on English forms.

(iii) Incorporation of English Terms

To attempt to give a glossary of English terms which have been added to Urdu vocabulary would seem not only idle but would add unnecessarily to the bulk of this work. Indeed our main line of procedure has all along been to rivet our attention on the tendencies and influences which have shaped modern Urdu literature rather than on the specific and minute details of their results. It is not material to our purpose to note what particular words and expressions from English have been introduced into Urdu, and they are innumerable. What we are, however, interested in is to know what *kind* of words have been imported and with what *object*.

In a country such as India, where, as pointed out in a preceding chapter, influences of a far-reaching character have been at work for nearly a hundred and fifty years, as the result of British administration, it is by no means strange that words and terms from English pertaining to administration in all its branches, *e. g.* governor, viceroy, officer, captain, major, colonel, doctor, surgeon, police, inspector, professor, principal, head-master, college, school, courts, judge, council, parliament, and municipality, to means of communication, *e. g.* road, railway, motor, bicycle, telegraph, post office; and to articles of English dress, as tie, collar, coat, pantaloon; to foreign machinery, *e. g.* engine, and to articles of consumption, *e. g.* biscuit, brandy, champagne and words descriptive of other miscellaneous things, more or less new to the country and particularly associated with English life, should have inevitably crept into the Urdu language and be in current use. What is more significant is the tendency among a large number of Urdu writers to employ, even in most serious compositions, without apology and with little effort at translation, literary or scientific terms and expressions from the English language.

There have not been wanting writers of distinction who have been looking with serious apprehension at this increasing influx of English terms into Urdu literature. The late Dr. Sayyid 'Alī Bilgirāmī was among the first to raise a protest. In the preface to his masterly translation of Le Bon's *La Civilisation des Arabes*, published in 1898 under the auspices of the "Dā,iratᵘ'l-Ma'ārif," subsidised by the Nizam's Government as one of the monumental series of Urdu works relating to India and Islam known as "Silsila-i-Āṣifiyya," of which Dr. Bilgirāmi was the editor, he observes:

"I have in this translation strenuously endeavoured to avoid the use of any English words, and to express the subject in simple and clear Urdu, so that it could be easily understood by everyone. No doubt a certain amount of care will be needed to understand those problems dealt with in the book which are by nature philosophic and abstruse. But as far as possible no confusion or ambiguity has been allowed to remain in the expression.

" For some years our new products of (English) schools, and to a certain extent our own elders of the community, have fallen into the habit of using unnecessarily such a considerable number of English words in their speeches and writings that, should the practice continue for some time longer, the Urdu language will become totally extinct, and in its place will rise a new language which will deserve to be styled not ' Urdu-i-Mu'alla,' or Excellent Urdu, but ' Urdu-i-Mārkaṭ,' or Urdu of the market-place."[1]

The reference to the elders of the community in the above passage is probably to the late Sir Sayyid Aḥmad and Ḥāfiẓ Naẕīr Aḥmad, who seem to have set the fashion. It will be interesting to know what they thought about the matter. Says Sir Sayyid Aḥmad in *Tahẕīb^{u}'l-Akhlāq* :[2]

" Some people complain that Urdu writers of the present day introduce English words into their writings. But they ought to understand that in a living language there is always a tendency to assimilate or form new and newer words. When a language gets exclusive or limited in range, it is considered a dead language. To naturalise foreign words is the work of the ' masters of the language.' But that is not an easy task. The ' masters of the language ' incorporate foreign words into their own language with the same excellent effect as the mosaic in the Tāj Maḥal. No doubt it is a different stone. But it is so united with the other that even after a close examination it does not seem to have been set into it, but appears to have grown out of it. This is not possible for any except the ' masters of the language,' and even then not by every ' master of language,' but only by those whom God has favoured with such a gift.

" It is also to be considered why the ' masters of the language ' feel the need for introducing foreign words. There are various reasons. A historian writing the history of a country often feels it necessary to retain certain terms peculiar to the organisation and political life of that country

[1] Special translation.
[2] See Vol. I, p. 490, Lahore, 1896.

which cannot be substituted by any terms which do not have the same association of ideas behind them. If you look into the histories of foreign countries which have been compiled in the Arabic language in Tunis, you will find what a large number of foreign words have been made use of. Look into the issues of the Arabic Journal *al-Jawā-ib* and you will find the same tendency. Read the holy Qur'ān itself. How many words from other languages have been employed therein? If modern terms had ceased to be imported into Arabic writings on arts and sciences, Arabic language would long ago have been numbered among the dead languages such as Zend and Sanskrit." [1]

It is not necessary to linger over the consideration which of the two attitudes is the more fruitful in literature. A great deal depends on the language, the writer's capacity for expression and the nature of the subject to be treated. Dr. Bilgirāmī's standpoint, which a few orthodox members of the Osmania University Translation Bureau have in common, may be profitable in certain special cases, but to assume a rigid attitude and refuse to use any English term, however more expressive than any newly coined equivalent in Urdu, is to stunt the growth of the language. After all, we should never forget the mixed origin of Urdu. Under the stress of modern life no language, whether of the East or of the West, can afford to remain free from outside influences.

(iv) New Forms of Prose Composition

We shall now pass on to consider the several forms which Urdu has borrowed from English literature. It has been already observed that as it is a quite new field, there has been nothing from the past to restrict movement. Indeed in the natural enthusiasm of youth it has so far left no form unattempted. But we propose to limit our con-

[1] Special translation.

sideration only to those in which anything in the character of literature has been produced.

They may be treated under the following heads : (1) Essay, (2) History, (3) Prose Fiction, (4) Drama, and (5) Literary Criticism.

Essay.—The term " Essay," as understood in English, is so elastic and covers such a variety of compositions, ranging from Bacon's brief notes full of " concentrated wisdom " to the most elaborate dissertations, such as Locke's *Essay Concerning Human Understanding*, Herbert Spencer's *Essay on Progress*, and even long biographical sketches by Macaulay and Carlyle, that it is futile to attempt to define its scope and character and define its form and features. We shall, for purposes of this inquiry, accept the term for what it means in common usage, for whatever definitions may have been offered from time to time, the broad fact ought not to be lost sight of, that in actual practice it has been found difficult to adhere rigidly to any one of them. In fact, as every essay is essentially the expression of a personal attitude towards any problem or theme, and as this personal element naturally differs with different writers, it will be not only arbitrary but positively injurious to the best interests of literary progress to reduce the idea of Essay to anything approaching precision.

Hence in Urdu prose we find a bewildering variety of compositions going under the common name of " Maẓmūn," or Essay. There is the translation of Bacon's Essays which have inspired a multitude of text-books, in some cases with an Oriental background to the thoughts expressed. There are the several hundreds of essays contributed primarily by the late Sir Sayyid Aḥmad K͟hān, poet Ḥālī, Nawwāb Muḥsinᵘ'l-Mulk and Sayyid Chirāg͟h 'Alī to the *Taḥẕībᵘ-'l-Ak͟hlāq*—a journal started avowedly in imitation of the *Tatler* and the *Spectator* of Addison and Steele. There are, again, the " speeches " and " lectures " of various literary and public men, chiefly those of Sir Sayyid Aḥmad and Ḥāfiẓ Naẕīr Aḥmad; the ambitious dissertations on religious, philosophic, historical and literary subjects, such as " Islam," by Mirzā G͟hulām Aḥmad Qādiyānī, " Propagation of Islam," by Nawwāb Muḥsinu'l-Mulk, Ḥālī's portentous preface to his poems dealing with the art of poesy, " *K͟huṭubāt-i-Aḥmadiyya*," or religious addresses, by Sir Sayyid Aḥmad, and *Darbār-i-Akbarī*, or the Court of Akbar, by Muḥammad Ḥusayn Āzād; various so-called Sawāniḥ or biographies treating of certain aspects of the lives of important historical personages, such as *al-Fārūq* of Shiblī, and *Ḥasan-bin-Ṣabbāḥ* of 'Abdu'l-Ḥalīm Sharar; the literary reviews by distinguished Urdu writers which have appeared from time to time in the leading periodicals, such as the *Mak͟hzan* (Magazine) of Lahore, the *Dilgudāz* of Lucknow, the *Adīb* of Allahabad, the *Urdu* of Aurangābād, and the allegorical writing, *Nayrang-i-K͟hiyāl* (Phenomenon of Imagination) of Āzād dealing with the problems of human life and drawing its inspiration from Greek mythological lore, all of which are essentially of the nature of Essay.

(v) Biography and History

Biography.—Under the title of " Sawāniḥ-i-'Umrī " or " Ḥayāt " or " Sīrat " or " Taẕkirah " or " Ḥālāt " or " Yādgār," numerous accounts of important historical personages, especially saints and religious preceptors, have been written since Urdu prose was evolved at the end of the eighteenth century. But the first serious biography on modern lines did not appear until 1886, when Ḥālī published his *Ḥayāt-i-Sa'dī* (Life of Sa'dī, the Persian poet). In the preface to his work, Ḥālī observes:

" The practice of writing accounts of the lives of distinguished personages known in Greek as ' Biography,' and in Arabic as ' *Taẕkira* ' or ' *Tarjuma*,' has been in vogue more or less from very ancient times. Although. in the early times, accounts of the deeds of heroes and of mythological gods were mostly committed to memory and narrated by word of mouth on special occasions, the Jews were accustomed to keep written records of the lives of their ancestors. The Greeks and Romans were the next to give their attention in this direction. So much so that the biographies written by the famous Roman Plutarch, who lived in the second century of the Christian era, are the best of the biographical accounts written in that age.

"In the early Christian literature there are accounts of the lives of the saints, martyrs, and reformers, which are to a certain extent complete in themselves. In the Middle Ages the most trustworthy biographies are those attempted by the Muslims. But in either of the two periods the general practice was to rely on tradition rather than on independent research, and indulge in exaggeration. The same tendency is also noticeable in the biographical accounts by Muslims. Only in the narration of the lives of those who have handed down the traditions of the Prophet, special care has been taken and the character of each—his shortcomings as well as his virtues—described with scrupulous regard to truth. For the rest, the biographies of theologians and poets are not so authentic. As biographical writing was based on hearsay, except when dealing with well-known historical personages, such as caliphs, sultans, ministers and military commanders, it was necessarily meagre. The life of not even one of the most distinguished writers (of Islam) has been treated properly.

"In *modern times*, particularly from the seventeenth century, European historians have brought the art of biographical writing to a state of perfection. So much so, that, as in history, there has been evolved a philosophy of biography. In modern biographies historical and scientific accuracy is insisted upon, and inferences are drawn from established facts. The work of the writer is subjected to thorough examination and his virtues or defects clearly indicated. Often several bulky volumes are devoted to each writer."[1]

Such then is the spirit in which Ḥālī conceived his biographical account of the life of Sa'dī.

"The book," as he explains, "is divided into two parts, followed by a conclusion. In the first part the facts of the

[1] Special translation.

Shaykh's (Sa'dī) life are given, in the second there is a detailed account of his works. In the conclusion his life and poetry as a whole has been critically reviewed."[1]

Two more biographies from the same pen appeared, *Yādgār-i-Ghālib* in 1897, and *Ḥayāt-i-Jāwīd* in 1901, the former being the life of his great master in poetry at whose feet he first began to "lisp in numbers," the latter of the friend, guide and inspirer of his middle and advanced years. These three biographies, together with some of those written by his contemporary, Mawlana Shiblī, which will presently be mentioned under History, form some of the best writings in Urdu literature.

History.—In this field two names stand out prominently —the late Muḥammad Ẕakāu'llah, sometime Professor of Mathematics, Muir Central College, Allahabad, and author of a monumental work in six volumes on the History of India, and Shiblī, the poet and historian, author of the *Shi'r^u'l-'Ajam*, or literary history of Persia, the *Sīrat^u'n-Nabī*, or the life of the Prophet, and of numerous historical sketches connected with the heyday of Islam, and the founder of the Nadwat^u'l 'Ulamā, or Theological College of Lucknow.

From the point of view of literature, Shiblī is of far greater importance to us.

Born in the year of the great Indian Mutiny (1857), at Azamgarh,[2] and passing the period of adolescence and youth in the traditional Islamic studies, he came early in life under the influence of Sir Sayyid Aḥmad and was for some years Professor of Arabic at the great seat of Islamic learning founded by him at Aligarh. It was at this place that he formed the friendship of Professor (Sir) Thomas Arnold, then occupying the Chair of Philosophy at the same College. What influence a man of the calibre of Shiblī would have exercised on the latter is beyond the scope of our present

[1] Special translation. [2] Shiblī died in 1914.

inquiry, but that Shiblī was profoundly influenced by him is borne out by the tender and affectionate references Shiblī makes of him in his *Safar-nāma-i-Rūm*, etc., and in his *Ṣubḥ-i-Umayd*. As Nizāmī-i-Badāyūnī in the preface to *Kashūf*[u]*'sh-Shamsayn* observes :

"Professor Arnold enlightened him (Shiblī) in modern principles (of literature). He explained to him the needs and requirements of modern literary life. He pointed out to him the lines of attack on ancient learning. Shiblī's intellectual acumen was of such high quality that he did not feel dazzled by the glamour of modern principles. He examined them coolly and with confidence. What was good in them he unhesitatingly accepted. Not only did he accept them, but he willingly let them be his guides in life. And what was artificial or ornamental he rigidly discarded."[1]

Shiblī is admittedly the greatest research scholar the Indian Musalmans have ever produced. His special field was early Islamic history.

"In modern times," says he, in his *Heroes of Islam*, "the art of historical writing has been brought to such a state of perfection, and the spirit of European scientific investigation has introduced so many scientific points into it, that our ancient (historical) works are insufficient for our purposes."

He then gives a list of the standard works in use among Muslims, and continues :

"These are the works which are considered the best among the books on Islamic history. But after reading all these, if we desire to know what in a particular reign was the state of civilisation, what the economic condition, what the laws and methods of administration, what the extent and sources of revenue, what the strength of the military forces, what the administrative posts, it will be difficult to get satisfaction even in one respect. In fact even when we should like to have an idea of the manners and customs prevalent in the time of the writer, we hardly obtain any details such as will raise a picture of that

[1] Special translation.

society before our minds. The facts described with needless elaboration, and for which thousands of pages have been sacrificed, are but these : coronation ceremonies, internecine quarrels, territorial conquests, rebellions, and appointments and dismissals of revenue officers. Even these are so superficially treated that it is impossible to determine the cause and effect of any event or to deduce any historical truths and inferences."[1]

The above explains the mind Shiblī brought to bear on his work, which he undertook as an almost religious duty. In a subsequent chapter we shall revert to this subject in order to describe the spirit in which he followed the principles he has laid down. At this stage we shall merely mention his principal writings.

His first important historical work is the *Royal Heroes of Islam* (in two parts), from which we have just quoted. It was published in 1888 and was followed by *Sīratᵘ'n-N'umān* (two parts, 1892) or the life and works of the great Sunni reformer Abū Ḥanīfa; *al-Fārūq* (two parts, 1899) or the life of the Caliph 'Umar; *al-Ghazālī* (1902) or the life of the Muslim philosopher of that name; *'Ilmᵘ'l Kalām* (1902) dealing with the history of scholastic theology amongst the Moslems; *al-Hārūn* and *al-Ma'mūn*, or the lives of the famous Hārunᵘ'r-Rashīd and his son Ma'mūn; *Sawāniḥ-i-'Umr-i-Mawlānā-i-Rūm* or the life of the great mystic poet of Persia, Jalālᵘ'd-Din Rūmī; *Shi'rᵘ'l-'Ajam* or the literary history of Persia; *Sīratᵘ'n-Nabī* or the life of the Prophet (left unfinished), and eleven historical essays written at different times but collected together and published in a single volume entitled *Rasā,il-i-Shiblī* in 1898.

At the present time there are innumerable works on history in the Urdu language, mostly translations and compilations, treating of almost every important country in the world. Some of them, particularly those written for the "Silsila-

[1] Special translation.

i-Āṣafiyya " and the Osmania University, Hyderabad, have a value of their own as handy text-books for use in colleges. But in the design and manner of execution few of them reach the standard of Shiblī's masterpieces.

(vi) Prose Fiction

The craving for light amusement such as is derivable from tales and stories is a universal feeling common to all races and grades of society. Among communities given to an easy life, such as the Indian Muslims of the nineteenth century, and with no preoccupations calling for strenuous action, this feeling is probably stronger and more pronounced. That seems to explain partly why the early prose literature in Urdu was so overloaded with tales and stories. It is significant that the very first efforts at prose writing made under the superintendence of Dr. Gilchrist were works on fiction.

Long before the art of story-telling was borrowed from English literature, innumerable stories fashioned on indigenous ideals had been written under diverse names in Urdu—" Afsāna," " Fasāna," " Qiṣṣa," " Kahānī," " Ḥikāyat," and " Tilism." Some of these, especially *Fasāna-i-'Ajāi,b*, *Ṭilism-i-Hūsh-Rubā*, *Būstān-i-Khayāl*, and *Dāstān-i-Amīr Ḥamzā*, at one time enjoyed considerable popularity.

These imaginative works are valuable to us for the reason that they have contributed to and in a measure even demonstrated the capacity of the Urdu language. Otherwise a large majority of them hardly have any human interest at all. The imagination to which they owe their birth is a kind of imagination whose peculiar virtue lies in bodying forth a world with which we have nothing in common—a world peopled by fairies and genii and strange and impossible human characters. Not that supernatural beings, such as the mind can create, should have no place in serious art.

If that were so, some of the best of Shakespearian works, for instance, would lose much of their attraction. The fault of the early works in Urdu prose fiction is not that the supernatural element is present in them, but that it is there without having any bearing on the passions, conflicts, problems, joys and sorrows which "belong to the essential texture of life." These imaginary beings are allowed to loom large on the canvas. In fact, they are the masters of it. Man as man has no place in the drama of their existence. Only the abnormal and the unnatural types are dragged into their midst merely to serve as a background to their unintelligible activities. Such a conception of life, however grotesque, may afford amusement and even deserve to be looked into with interest were it the subject of treatment in one or two works and presented with due regard to the requirements of plot-structure and characterisation. When, however, it becomes the be-all and end-all of almost every effort in fiction by writer after writer, and the mind refuses to seek out themes of greater human interest from the innumerable directions open to it, one is forced to the conclusion that the early story-tellers in Urdu did not understand the functions and qualifications of their art.

The first attempt in Urdu at anything approaching our conception of the modern novel, with dialogue playing a large part, was *Fasāna-i-Āzād*, by Ratan Nāth Sarshār, which appeared as a serial in his magazine, the *Awadh Akhbār*, December 1878–December 1879. It is a work of extraordinary length, written partly in prose and partly in verse. In simplicity of diction and charm of style, and in the portrayal of the social life and manners of the time, it is indeed an undoubted advance over the earlier works of fiction. But it must be admitted that it lacks the essential qualities of a novel, both in unity of plot and consistency of characterisation.

Since the publication of Ratan Nāth's *Fasāna-i-Āzād*

the art of story-telling has greatly improved in the hands of the writers of Urdu fiction. Not only have a good many tales and stories been translated from English, such as *Grimm's Fairy Tales*, *Æsop's Fables*, Lamb's *Tales from Shakespeare*, Dr. Johnson's *History of Rasselas*, Jules Verne's *From the Earth to the Moon*, Sir Walter Scott's *The Bride of Lammermoor* and *The Talisman*, and Marie Corelli's *Vendetta* and *The Soul of Lilith*, but innumerable original works modelled on the English novel have been produced.

A considerable majority of them are novelettes of the cheap sensational type we find to-day. Very few of these have any definite setting—social or historical—to their themes. They appeal to the less educated and more ignorant and credulous section of the people.

Of the rest which possess any literary value are the social novels, *Mir,āt^u'l-'Urūs*, *Banāt^u'n-Na'ash*, *Ibn^u'l-Waqt*, *Muḥṣināt*, *Tawbat^u'n-Naṣūḥ*, *Ayāma*, and *Ru'yā-i-Ṣādiqā* of Hāfiẓ Naẕīr Aḥmad K͟hān, and *Subḥ Zindagī* and *Shām-i-Zindagī* of Rāshid^u'l-K͟hayrī, and *Umraū Jan Ada*, *Ẕāt-i-Sharīf* and *Sharīf Zāda̱* of Mīrzā Muḥammad Hādī Ruswā, and the historical novels of *Ḥasan Angilina*, *Malik^u'l-'Azīz aur Virgina*, *Manṣūr awr Mohanā*, *Ziyād aur Halāwā*, *Ayyām-i-'Arab* and *Flora Florinda* of Muḥammad 'Abd^u'l-Ḥalīm Sharar.

Of these, Ḥāfiz Naẕīr Aḥmad Khān and Muḥammad 'Abd^u'l-Ḥalīm Sharar deserve special mention. As a prominent leader of the Aligarh movement, especially on its literary side, as the best translator of the Qur'ān in Urdu, and author of various essays and " lectures " ranking among the finest of literary productions, Ḥāfiẓ Naẕīr Aḥmad K͟hān will hold for many a year to come an honoured place among the foremost writers in Urdu, and may even outlive them, but as a novelist he must be given an inferior position to that of Sharar.

Naẕīr Aḥmad's novels are novels with a purpose, intended

specially for the women-folk, and calculated to bring home to them the social evils to which they are subject. Each novel is practically a collection of essays of different length expressed through the machinery of dialogue on the several aspects that arise out of the central theme. There is practically no love affair in any of these, for the writer avoided it out of deference to the prevailing moral sentiment that love stories should not be placed in the hands of the gentler sex !

Sharar's novels, on the other hand, are conceived in a different spirit—the spirit common to the English novelists. His works are evidently inspired by and modelled on those of Sir Walter Scott. Like Scott, Sharar went back to the romantic past of his own people, and endeavoured to vitalise it for the sake of his own generation. With a better knowledge of English literature, and better acquaintance with English life than was possible for Naẕīr Aḥmad, he seems to have understood the secrets of plot construction better than the other, although in the delineation of character and the faithful portrayal of human life he has his own serious defects, as we shall have occasion to notice later on in another connection. Here we shall merely point out that at the present stage in the development of the Urdu novel, Sharar enjoys a leading position and possesses a large number of imitators among the present-day novelists, and has, by his wider appeal, popularised, more than any other writer, the idea of the novel among the Urdu-speaking people of India.

(vii) Drama

The Drama, like the Novel, has been an entirely new acquisition to Urdu literature. Like music, the dramatic representation of life was always discouraged among orthodox Islamic communities, for the theologians regarded both the arts as profane. That was probably the reason why the foremost poets in Persian and Arabic left that field untouched. The instinct for music has now and then been allowed to assert itself under some religious pretext or other.[1] Indeed the Mogul Emperors of Delhi, with the solitary exception of Awrangzayb, were great patrons of this fine art. But with drama it was otherwise. It never could find its legitimate place in the social life of the Muslims.

Of all the countries inhabited by Muslim races, India was the place where the Muslims might easily have taken to dramatic writing as they did to music. For centuries the drama had been a recognised and honoured section of Hindu literature. The Moslem writers had everything at hand to inspire them to apply their genius in that direction. But they did not, and in fact would not; and this not because the theologians would condemn them. They had patronised Indian music in spite of the theologians. It was not, therefore, any religious scruple that stood in their way. It was the absence of example by any of their beau ideals—the Persian poets. What their masters did not, they as loyal followers would not do.

It was only when the last vestiges of Islamic power and glory were fast vanishing from India, at the indolent and effeminate Court of the last remnant of the dynasty of the Wazirs of Oudh, Wājid 'Alī Shāh, that the poet Amānat 'Alī Amānat wrote in rhymed verse what might be called the first opera in Urdu, the *Indar Sabhā*. It is interesting to notice that *Amānat* had not the courage to lend his name openly to this production for fear of the orthodox critics, for none of the earlier poets had written anything so new and unauthorised by the Persian poets.

This *Indar Sabhā*, or the assembly of Indra, the King of Fairies, is a drama of love between Gulfām and a fairy, Sabz Parī. It was written at the instance of King Wājid 'Alī Shāh, and staged at his private gatherings. When he

[1] Among certain Sufi orders music of a certain description called *sam'* or "sacred music" is allowed.

was deposed and the kingdom of Oudh annexed to British India, the play came to be produced before a wider public.

The next attempt at dramatic writing in Urdu was made under the auspices of the several Gujārātī theatrical companies equipped on modern lines which were established in Bombay about the close of the last century, under the management of enterprising Parsis, prominent among whom was a certain person by name Kaūsjī Pālanjī Khatāū. *Āb-i Iblīs, Anjām-i Ulfat, 'Āshiq-i Ṣādiq, Bī-naẓīr Badr-i Munīr, Layla Majnūn*, and *Sitam-i Hamanna* are some of those written for Khatāū. They were originally in Gujārātī character, for the actors and actresses, though conversant with the colloquial Urdu speech, were ignorant of the Persian aphabet in which Urdu was usually written.

These plays are in two to five acts, divided into scenes of varying length, and are expressly called "drama." They are not of much importance to us because, although the titles *Āb-i Iblīs, Anjām-i Ulfat* and so on are in the approved Urdu style, the language in the text is not Urdu properly so called. It is a mixture of some of those allied dialects which Sir Charles Lyall groups under the common name of Hindustani.[1]

Since these were written, various new productions have appeared, some of which, such as *Mahābhāratā, Sakuntalā* and *Harischandrā*, embody Indian tales and stories already known to the public through other channels. But a large number are adaptations from Shakespeare. They are called by the writers themselves, translations, but are, strictly speaking, adaptations. The stories are essentially the same in substance, but in the execution the great master's touch is lost. The names are all Oriental; the scenes are laid in the East. The very atmosphere is charged with ideas of Eastern life.

[1] See *Encycl. Brit.*, 11th. Ed., Vol. XIII., "Hindustani Literature."

Of the plays of Shakespeare which have been adapted in Urdu are *Romeo and Juliet*, *Hamlet*, *Othello*, *King Lear*, *Merchant of Venice*, *The Comedy of Errors*, *As You Like It*, *Midsummer Night's Dream*, *Love's Labour's Lost*, *Winter's Tale*, *Cymbeline* and *Tempest*.

We may mention here the more important adaptations of each.

Romeo and Juliet.—Āghā Muḥammad Shāh Ḥashr who seems to have understood the principles underlying Shakespearian art better than others, wrote his *Bazm-i Fānī* (Vanishing Assembly) in 1900 based on the story of *Romeo and Juliet*. It was followed by *Romeo and Juliet Mashhūr Gulnār Fīrūz* of Mahdi Ḥasan Khān in 1902, and by *'Ishq-i-Fīrūz Liqā wa Gulnār Siyar* of Mīrzā Naẓīr Bayg in 1905.

Hamlet.—There are four known versions of this in Urdu—*Jahāngīr, or Hamlet*, 1895, by Umrāu 'Alī; *Khūn-i Nāḥaq* (Futile Bloodshed), 1901, by Mahdī Ḥasan Khān, and *Wāqi'a-i Jahāngīr-i Nāshād*, 1904, by Mīrzā Naẓīr Bayg.

Othello and *King Lear.*—The story of Othello has been closely followed in *Ja'far* of Munshī Aḥmad Ḥusayn Khān, published in 1895, and of King Lear in a play of the same name by Lālā Sītārām, 1893.

The Merchant of Venice.—An anonymous adaptation of this entitled *Chānd Shāh Sawdāgar* (Chānd Shāh, the Merchant) appeared at Lahore in 1895, and another version by Shaykh 'Āshiq Ḥusayn, *Venice Kā Sawdāgar* (Merchant of Venice), at Lucknow in 1898.

The Comedy of Errors.—There are two so-called translations of this under one and the same title, *Bhūl Bulayyān*, one by Fīrūz Shāh Khān, Murādābād, 1896, and another by Lālā Sītārām, Murādābād, 1906.

Of the rest which deserve mention are *Jām-i Ulfat* (Midsummer Night's Dream), 1903, *Dilpizīr* (As You Like It), 1901, *Murīd-i Shakk* (Winter's Tale), 1900, *Yārān kī*

Miḥnat Barbād (Love's Labour's Lost), 1899, and *Tīr-i Nigāh* (Tempest), 1897.

It must be noticed that none of these playwrights enjoys any recognised place among men of letters. For the traditional prejudice against drama still persists in the orthodox literary circles. Had men of approved standing in other departments of literature applied their hand to drama, much of this prejudice might ere long have died out. As it happened, dramatic writing attracted to itself persons who are not, with the possible exception of Āghā' Ḥashr, even known to the general public by name. Their plays are rarely read even by those who frequent the theatre. They go there in order to witness the spectacular display on the stage and to listen to the music rather than to follow the action of the play with any intelligent interest. The stage is still intended for the crowd and the respectable classes fight shy of associating themselves with it. Unless literary men of real standing come forward to cultivate a taste for dramatic writing and produce plays worthy of being recognised as real literature, and unless educated persons shake off this age-long prejudice and join the stage, there seems to be little likelihood of drama taking its legitimate place in the life of Muslim society in India.

(viii) Literary Criticism

Alongside of these several new forms of writing in Urdu prose there has also grown a body of literature with the express object of interpreting literature. It is necessarily small in quantity, for not many years have passed since the "Renaissance" has set in, and much has yet to be done before literary critics can usefully look back and take stock of all that has been achieved. Their present efforts, therefore, have been directed not so much to examine and appraise the new enterprise in Urdu literature as to give a right lead to it, informed by the spirit and ideals of English literature.

This educative work in literary taste was first conceived and undertaken as a serious national duty by the leader of the Aligarh movement—Sir Sayyid Aḥmad K͟hān, who started the *Tahẕībᵘ'l-Ak͟hlāq* on the lines of the *Spectator* and the *Tatler* of Addison and Steele, and to which among others the poet Ḥālī very largely contributed.

As pointed out elsewhere, the literary activity of the last fifty years owes much of its inspiration and guidance to this journal, one of whose main functions was to purify the literary taste of the Muslim community, which had long been vitiated under the influence of Persian literature. The *Tahẕībᵘ'l-Ak͟hlāq* relentlessly exposed all that was artificial and insincere in the old literature, and enlightened the Muslim literary public on the principles which encourage and sustain all true literature. The ideal that it held out before them was the masterpieces of English literature. How far this ideal has appealed to the Urdu writers and been followed in regard to form and technique we have already tried to explain. In the words of Ḥālī, it has "revolutionised their conception of literature." The services of the *Tahẕībᵘ'l-Ak͟hlāq* in the field of literary criticism cannot thus be over-rated. Its work has been supplemented since by the masterly prologomena of Ḥālī to his poetical works, in which he deals with the art of poetry as understood in the East and in the West, and sums up the essentials which have been recognised on all hands as forming the life and substance of all good poetry. The monumental historical and critical survey of Persian poetry, *Shi'rᵘ'l-'Ajam* by Shiblī, the prefaces of Ḥālī and other writers of the front rank to their different works, and the reviews and magazine articles published from time to time in the leading Urdu periodicals, have carried on the work of the *Tahzīb^u'l-Akhlāq* and in some measure succeeded in educating the public taste for literary appreciation.

In recent years, owing largely to political causes, such as the growth of nationalism in India and the rise of the pan-Islamic spirit, it has become the fashion with the younger school of Muslim literary critics to glorify and exalt the leading Urdu poets out of all proportion to their intrinsic worth. As an illustration of the extravagant lengths to which even intelligent and otherwise highly cultured persons would go in their blind eulogy of their favourite authors may be mentioned the *Appreciation of Ghālib* by the late 'Abdu'r-Rahmān Bijnawrī, a Doctor of Philosophy of Göttingen, contributed to the *Urdu*, a magazine expressly devoted to the refinement of literary taste among its readers. With an *obiter dictum* at the head of his review, that "There are only two inspired books in India—the Sacred Vedās, and the Dīwān of Ghālib," he proceeds to compare his idol in one or other of his qualities with almost every figure known to him in European art, literature and philosophy, like Giotto, Lorenzetti, Raphael, Rubens; Virgil, Ariosto, Goethe, Mombert, Millarme, Rimbaud, Victor Hugo, Mademoiselle De Maupin, Verlaine, Maeterlinck, Ibsen; Shakespeare, Wordsworth, Fitzgerald; Kant, Hegel, Spinoza, Bacon, Berkeley, Spencer, Darwin, Wallace, Laplace, Lodge, Haeckel, Herschel, and Fichte. Such an imposing array of names, far from helping an understanding of the qualities of Ghālib's mind and art, has, if anything, served to obscure them. No attempt is made to form a judicious estimate of the author by showing his characteristic defects equally with his distinctive merits as a poet. Moreover, the extracts from German and French writers designed to bring out by comparison or contrast the peculiar virtues of Ghālib were not translated for the benefit of the readers, who were mostly ignorant of those languages. After reading this lengthy review, one is still left in doubt as to what really constitutes Ghālib's greatness as a poet.

Of a piece with this method of literary criticism is the observation of the learned editor himself, who commends such a review in the following terms :

"For force of expression, acuteness of observation, and loftiness of ideas, this contribution is something quite new in Urdu literature."[1]

More pardonable but equally undiscriminating is the estimate in English of the poet Iqbāl by Sir Zūlfiqār 'Alī Khān, a nobleman of Malayrkotla, who prefaces the work with this luminous remark :

"If the Peacock Throne is the pride of Persia, and the lustrous Kohinoor the glory of the British Crown, Iqbāl would surely adorn the court of the Muses in any country."

This style of literary criticism, wholly laudatory and delightfully vague, is, we venture to think, but a recrudescence of the old spirit when writers for one reason or other, whether from self-interest, personal attachment or sheer lack of discernment, did not respond to the true requirements of their art. But with the spread of education and the growth of an intelligent and discriminating literary public, literary criticism should normally assume a truer perspective, and the standard set by Ḥālī in accordance with the best traditions of the West prevail and further the cause of true literature.

(ix) Recapitulation

As the result of the influences which have been at work, and which we have in the preceding pages tried to analyse and describe, Urdu literature has taken a new turn altogether. No longer is it confined to verse, and no longer is that verse

[1] Special translation.

hedged in by meaningless and artificial restrictions such as had clogged the freedom of thought and expression in the past. A new and vigorous and expansive prose has taken its rise where there was none before, and has already invaded every department of literature legitimately falling within its purview, bearing on it the impress of English literature which inspired its growth and formation.

In the next chapter we propose to take this new literature as a whole, and try to get behind it and sift the main ideas and ideals which it has embodied and for which it stands.

CHAPTER VII

NEW MATTER AND SPIRIT

When we look into the new Urdu literature and examine its spirit and content, certain broad ideas meet our eye at almost every turn which seem to have inspired and stimulated its growth, and around which the entire body of literature apparently revolves, ideas which from their character and expression suggest their unmistakable indebtedness to English literature.

(i) Spirit of Freedom

Prominent among these stands out the spirit of freedom in all its bearings which English life and English literature, particularly of the nineteenth century, has stood for—the spirit which has generated those ideas lying at the root of all the movements in England intended to promote the cause of democracy and political liberty, of social freedom and equality, of religious tolerance and freedom of conscience, and of freedom from literary convention and intellectual bondage, which have one and all, in one form or another, travelled to India and found expression in its literature.

This expression has varied with different communities according to their capacity for assimilation and reaction.

As Urdu literature is essentially a Muslim contribution, we are particularly concerned with the thought and life and activity of the Muslim community as reflected therein.

Ideas of Political Freedom.—We have already seen the abject helplessness to which the Muslims of India had been reduced as the result of the series of political misfortunes culminating in the Great Indian Mutiny and the consequent extinction of the Mogul Empire. Suspected by the British rulers for their supposed complicity in the revolt, outdistanced in the race of intellectual and material progress by the sister Hindu community, the Muslims who had no alternative but to suppress whatever political aspiration they might have had, and pursue a policy calculated to preserve their political existence against the encroachments of the Hindu community—a policy which necessarily drove them into the camp of those who had deprived them of their political domination in the country, but who were credited with the power and the sense of justice and fair play to protect such of their legitimate interests and aspirations as did not prejudice the safety and stability of the empire. Hence from 1858 down to the close of the nineteenth century and even after, till 1909, when the Morley-Minto reforms were inaugurated in the administration of the country, the attitude of the Muslims towards political problems was one of trust and confidence in the British rulers based on a frank exposition and representation of their aims which, as they conceived, would keep them immune from the "tyranny" of the majority. It was clearly a movement for freedom, though it was freedom compromised by the aforesaid restrictions and considerations.

Opinions might differ as to whether such an attitude was truly patriotic. In fact there were not wanting men in the foremost ranks of Hindu society who stigmatised it as reactionary and anti-national. But the question deserving of consideration is whether the advanced political aspirations in which the prosperous Hindu intelligentsia were indulging could have suited an educationally and economically backward community such as the Muslims of the last generation undoubtedly were, and whether they *as a community* would not have suffered by an unequal alliance with those more favourably placed in the struggle for political advancement. The primary concern of the Muslims was the spreading of knowledge and enlightenment as a preparation for a fuller enjoyment of common political liberty. Hence they concentrated all their energy and attention on their education and left all questions of communal political safety in the hands of the British Government, whom they, however, kept fully informed from time to time in the frankest manner possible of their needs and grievances. From the standpoint of the Hindu political programme the attitude of the Indian Muslims might appear reactionary, but from that of the Muslims themselves it was but an expression of their desire to have a free and unimpeded path for progress along their own lines.

This attitude and this conception of liberty and freedom is reflected not only in the writings of Sir Sayyid Aḥmad, its chief exponent and advocate, but also in those of the leading poets and prose writers of the last half of the nineteenth century, such as Ḥālī, Āzād, Naẕīr Aḥmad, Muḥsinu'l-Mulk and Justice Sayyid Maḥmūd.

For a clearer understanding of this idea of political freedom we may be permitted to quote two extracts from Sir Sayyid Aḥmad.

Writing in his *Causes of the Indian Mutiny* (1858),[1] he draws attention to certain fundamental principles which should be kept in view in the good governance of a dependency, the neglect of which was at the root of all the troubles of 1857. Says he:

"The primary causes of rebellion are, I fancy, everywhere the same. It invariably results from the existence of a policy obnoxious to the dispositions, aims, habits and views of those by whom the rebellion is brought about.

"Most men agree in thinking that it is highly conducive to the welfare and prosperity of Government—indeed, is essential to its stability—that the people should have a voice in its councils. It is from the voice of the people only that

[1] A translation of it in English by Sir Auckland Colvin and Col. G. F. J. Graham appeared in 1873.

Government can learn whether its projects are likely to be well received. The voice of the people can alone check errors in the bud, and warn us of dangers before they burst upon and destroy us.

"A needle may dam the gushing rivulet: an elephant must turn aside from the swollen torrent. This voice, however, can never be heard, and this security never acquired unless the people are allowed a share in the consultations of Government. The men who have ruled India should never have forgotten that they were here in the position of foreigners—that they differed from its natives in religion, in customs, in habits of life and of thought. The security of a Government is founded on its knowledge of the character of the governed, as well as on its careful observance of their rights and privileges. They are in every instance the inheritance of the peculiar race. It is to the differences of thought and of custom that laws must be adapted, for they cannot be adapted to the laws. In their due observance lies the welfare and security of Government. From the beginning of things, to disregard these has been to disregard the nature of man, and the neglect of them has ever been the cause of universal discontent."

With this fearless exposition of the functions of Government as he conceived them, there always went a strong and earnest appeal to his people to understand their duties to themselves and to Government. In one of his speeches he observes :—

"Mr. John Stuart Mill, in his able work on Political Economy, says: 'The rights and interests of every or of any person are only secure from being disregarded when the person interested is himself able and habitually disposed to stand up for them. The second is that the general prosperity attains a greater height, and is more widely diffused, in proportion to the personal energies enlisted in promoting it.' These principles, my friends, are as applicable to the people of India as they are to those of any other nation; and it is in your power, it now rests with you alone, to put them into practice. If you will not help yourselves, you may be quite certain no one else will. . . . Be loyal in your hearts, place every reliance upon your rulers, speak out openly, honestly and respectfully all your grievances, hopes and fears, and you may be quite sure that such a course of conduct will place you in the enjoyment of all your legitimate rights; and that this is compatible, nay, synonymous with true loyalty to the State, will be upheld by all whose opinion is worth having."

Such was the attitude of the Muslim community in political matters as reflected in their activity and literature down to the close of the last century. But with the beginning of the new century, however, there came about a great change in their political outlook. The gradual disappearance of the leaders of the last generation, and the consciousness and awakening born of enlightenment and modern English education, gave rise to new interests and new ideals. No longer was their concern for political safety and freedom confined to themselves in India, but began to cover a much wider field, to wherever their co-religionists lived—Turkey, Persia, Turkestan, Egypt, Tripoli, Morocco and even China. This feeling of extra-territorial interest in brethren of the same faith, sometimes described as "Pan-Islamism," was intensified with the final dismemberment of the Turkish Empire, beginning with the Italian invasion of Tripoli in 1911, and followed soon after by the conflagration in the Balkans and ending in the tragedy of the late war, and found expression in an endless number of pamphlets, magazine and newspaper articles, poems and speeches, by writers and speakers of all sorts and conditions, prominent among whom may be mentioned, Iqbāl, Shiblī, Abū'l-Kalām Āzād, Ḥasrat Muhānī, Ẓafar 'Alī K͟hān, Muḥammud 'Alī, Shawkat 'Alī, and 'Abdu'l-Majīd Sharar.

To go behind this particular section of Urdu literature and analyse the feelings and motives underlying the productions of each leading writer would be an unpleasant and difficult task. In the first place the material is not fully available; almost all of it appeared in the daily newspaper; some of it was proscribed and confiscated by Government.

In the second place a considerable portion of it was not spontaneous, but written for propaganda purposes, and therefore could hardly be acceptable as an index to the personality of the writers, for the quality of their writings has changed with the changing methods and tactics of their mission.

We may, however, indicate the broad aspects of this Pan-Islamic feeling in India as reflected in their literature, especially in the writings of poets like Iqbal and Shiblī, who, living outside of the regular propaganda activity, have nevertheless given expression to the disquiet that seized the mind of the Indian Muslim community during the last few years.

This feeling expressed itself in three different ways: sorrow over the loss of freedom or power of any Islamic race, whether in the distant past or the present; concern about the future of the Islamic countries subject to European political influences; and suspicion and distrust of European nations who, in the opinion of the writers, had brought about the downfall of Muslim rule everywhere.

Dr. Iqbāl was for some time considered the chief exponent of this phase of political Islam. It is stated that once passing through the Straits of Messina on a voyage to England, he happened to cast his eyes on the Sicilian coast. The sight moved him. It reminded him of the days when the Arabs once held sway in that island. The thought threw him apparently into an emotional anguish :—

"Weep to thy heart's content, O blood-weeping eye,
Yonder is visible the grave of Muslim culture.
Once this place was the tent of those dwellers of the desert,
For whose ships the ocean was a playground,
Who raised earthquakes in the courts of mighty emperors,
In whose sabres lay hidden life-scorching flames,
Whose birth tolled the knell of effete ideals,
With whose fear the strongholds of falsehood trembled,
Whose electric touch revived life into the world,
And broke the chains of superstition.

"Once thou wast the cradle of the civilisation of this race,
The fire of whose glance was world-captivating beauty.
The nightingales of Shīrāz wailed over Baghdad;
And Dāgh wept tears of blood over Delhi.
When the heavens scattered the wealth of Granada to the winds,
The saddened heart of Ibn Badrūn raised its plaintive cry.
To sing the dirge of thy ruin was to fall to my lot;
This torture—yea, self-torture was reserved for me.
Tell me of thy anguish; I too am full of pain;
I am the dust raised by that caravan which once broke its journey here.
Paint to me that picture of the old,
Rouse me by telling the tale of bygone days;
And I shall carry thy gift to India,
And make others weep as I weep now."[1]

In his *Shikwa*, or "Complaint to God," he seems to ask: Why are the Muslim races in the throes of misery?

"There are nations besides us: there are sinners amongst them too,
Humble folk and those intoxicated with pride,
Slothful, careless or clever,
Hundreds there are who are tired of Thy Name.
But Thy Grace descends on their dwellings
And the lightning strikes but ours.

'Gone are the Muslims'; so the idols in the temples say:
And rejoice that the protectors of the *Ka'ba* are no more,
'The world's stage is cleared of the camel drivers,
With their Qur'ān in their armpits have they fled.'
The polytheists are laughing at us. Hast Thou no feeling?
Hast Thou no regard for Thy Unity?"[2]

From the condition of the Muslim races, he looks at those who, he considers, have brought about their downfall, and makes a significant gesture at them.[3]

"The time of unveiling has come, the beloved will be seen by all,
The secret which was veiled by silence shall now become manifest.
That cycle of the cup-bearer has gone when the lovers of wine drank in hiding;
The whole world shall now become a tavern, and all shall drink in the open.

---

[1] See *A Voice from the East*, by Sir Zūlfiqār 'Alī Khān, Lahore, 1922, pp. 27–29. With the exception of a few lines the whole passage as translated therein has been entirely recast here in order to bring out the spirit of Iqbāl's original.

[2] Special translation. [3] *A Voice from the East.*

For, the silence of Mecca has proclaimed to the expectant ear at last,
That the compact made with the desert dwellers shall be strengthened again.

The lion which emerged out of the wilderness and upset the Empire of Rome,
I hear from the angels that he shall awaken once more.

O dwellers of Western lands, God's world is not a shop;
That which you considered good coin shall prove to be counterfeit.

'Your civilisation will commit suicide with its own dagger,
A nest built on a slender bough is not secure.'"[1]

"(The poem beginning Zamāna āyā hai bī-ḥijābī kā," etc.)

In his "Reply" to the *Shikwā* he strikes the same note.

The trouble that is raging in the Balkans
Is a message of awakening to the forgetful.
Thou may'st think it the means of vexing thy heart.
But in reality it is a test of thy self-sacrifice and self-reliance.
Why art thou frightened at the neighing of the enemy's horse?
Truth's light can never be put out by the breath of the enemy."[2]

More bitter is the tone of Shiblī's sorrow over the misfortunes and loss of power and freedom of his co-religionists. It is an unmitigated sorrow without any ray of hope. In his *Hangāma-i-Balqān* (The Trouble in the Balkans), written a few years before he died, he gives expression to rank pessimism, and his denunciation of the European attitude is all the more forceful because it is so full of restraint.

"When decline has set in over political power, the name and banner will stand—how long?

The smoke from the burnt candle of a vanished assembly will rise—how long?

When the sky has torn the mantle of power to pieces,
Its shreds will float in the air—how long?

Gone is Morocco, gone is Persia. We have now to see
This helpless 'sick man of Turkey' will live—how long?

This tide of woe which is advancing from the Balkans,
The sighs of the oppressed will stem—how long?

---

[1] See *A Voice from the East*. [2] Special translation.

Will someone ask, ye teachers of civilisation,
How long these cruelties, these atrocities—how long?

How long this provoking hurricane of injustice and trouble?
This delight at wailing and crying—how long?

How long will ye take vengeance for the victory of Ayyūb?
Ye will show us the sight of the crusaders—how long?

The decline of the rule of 'Uṣmān is the decline of religion.
Friends! the thought of son and wife and property—how long?

In God's Name, do ye understand what these preparations are?
If ye have not understood now, you will fail to understand—how long?

If the worshippers of the dust of *Ka'ba* disappear,
Then will last the sanctity of the angel-hallowed place—how long?

When the fowler's gaze is towards the Holy Place,
The nests of its birds are safe—how long?

Shiblī! should you long to migrate, where can you go now?
Syria or Najd or Cyrene are sanctuaries—how long?" [1]

Such then is the spirit of a large body of literature that has been put forth during recent years. A large portion of it is the expression of the moment of heat and excitement. In fact, except for a few poems, the literature of this brief period was neither intended to, nor did it, live beyond the few hours which are usually allowed to the sheets of evening newspapers. When the excitement dies out and things settle down to normal conditions, and a broader and bolder outlook takes hold of the people, especially of its intelligent section, what little of it has survived so far may probably be neglected and forgotten. We have referred to it and tried to analyse its features merely to illustrate the nature of reaction to English ideas of political freedom and liberty that has set in in the Indian Muslim community and is reflected in their Urdu literature.

Social and Religious Freedom.—To trace the spirit of freedom in the sphere of social and religious life, it should

[1] Special translation.

be made clear at the very outset that the literature in Urdu dealing with this aspect of the question is not, as in the political sphere, the expression or the reflection of the actual life of the people. It has not grown out of it, but has been superimposed by a handful of writers imbued with Western conceptions and anxious to influence the mind of the Muslim community to throw off the shackles of convention and tradition which had contributed in such large measure to the disintegration of their social and religious life, as already described at some length in a previous chapter.

Hence, these writings, whether dealing with the broad aspects of religion as *Khutabāt-i-Aḥmadiyyā* of Sir Sayyid Aḥmad, *Islām* of Mīrzā Ghulām Aḥmad Qādiyānī, and *'Ilmu'l-Kalām* of Shiblī, or with the socio-religious problems, as the *Tahzību'l-Akhlāq* of Sir Sayyid Aḥmad *Musaddas*, and *Bīwa-Kī-Munājāt* of Ḥālī, *Rū'yā-i-Ṣādiqā* of Nazīr Aḥmād Khān, or with particular social or religious questions as various social novels, especially of Nazir Aḥmād Khān and essays, lectures and poems of Ḥālī, Shiblī, Āzād, Zakāu'llah, Muḥsinu'l-Mulk and others are to be considered not as an expression of the communal life of the Indian Muslims, but as writings embodying the spirit and ideals held out to them for assimilation and guidance in order that they might work out their social regeneration on sound and healthy lines.

When we analyse the attitude of these several writers who one and all, with the exception of Mīrzā Ghulām Aḥmad Qādiyānī, cluster round the figure of Sir Sayyid Aḥmad, it seems to us that the primary question to which they addressed themselves was how far and why were the early theologians such as the *Imāms* Abū Ḥanīfa, Shāfi'ī, Mālik and Ḥanbal and others better entitled to interpret the dogma and tenets and social laws of Islam as laid down in the *Qur'ān* and the Prophet's sayings than anybody else, and why their interpretation should be binding on the Muslims for all time to come? Hence they refused to follow blindly their lead, and taking for their support the text of one of the Prophet's sayings that we must move with time, for God is Time, they tried to establish from the *Qur'ān* and the life of the Prophet and his immediate followers and successors that the ideas which governed the social life of modern Europe as represented in England were essentially Islamic ideals which they should imitate and follow as a serious religious obligation. In the *Tahẕību'l-Akhlāq*, which has been the most potent instrument of awakening, Sir Sayyid Aḥmad observes:

"Religious learning among us is spoiled to a degree. The commands of God which that innocent, simple-minded, truthful and sweet-natured Prophet had communicated to the ignorant and illiterate dwellers of the desert in such simple, clear and sincere manner have been so much distorted by such unwarranted importations into them of empty distinctions and subtleties, metaphysical propositions and arguments of logic that their original simplicity has ceased to make its appeal, with the result that the Muslims have been obliged to neglect the real commands contained in the *Qur'ān* and the authentic sayings, and to follow those invented by X, Y and Z."[1]

So great was the hold on the Muslim community of these later distortions of their religious and social ideals, and so bigoted were they, that the attempt of Sir Sayyid, Ḥālī and others to free their minds from this age-long bondage was met by most violent and undignified opposition. Still these earnest men did not slacken their energy, but went boldly forward in the sincere hope and trust that one day their voice would be heard, although at the time it was no better than the voice in the wilderness. This mixed feeling is painfully voiced in one of the issues of the *Tahẕību'l-Akhlāq*, which, as we have already pointed out, was a journal modelled expressly on the *Spectator* and *Tatler* of Addison and Steele.

[1] Special translation.

"Steele and Addison were fortunate that their contemporaries used to read and appreciate their writings. But our misfortune is that our writings are regarded as anti-religious. To read them is to court perdition. Steele and Addison used to throw off the effect of their day's toil and labour on listening to the quick applause which followed the publication of each issue of their paper; whereas on the publication of our paper we do not expect anything but curses and condemnation. Steele and Addison used to hear kind words from those to whom they rendered kind services. We, on the other hand, receive unkind things in return for kind deeds. It was not difficult for Steele and Addison to win over a thousand hearts. But to us it is extremely hard to captivate a single one. The task for Steele and Addison was to attract but ready-made and willing hearts. We, on the other hand, have to create the hearts before we can attract them.

"The public stigmatise our views as an expression of insanity and hypochondria. But there is method in our madness: we know what we are doing. Having regard to what has been so far achieved in this brief period, we trust in God and look forward to greater results; and prophesy that better days are ahead of us. When these will come we do not know. But come they must, we are perfectly certain in our mind.

"We do not say that by the help of this feeble organ we shall be able to do for India what Steele and Addison did in their days to England; but we say this, that to the best of our ability we will go on discharging our duty.

"'We but try to begin; it is for Him to complete.'"[1]

Although these hopes of the *Tahẕību'l-Aḵẖlāq* are yet far from being realised, still, it should be acknowledged that the awakening which this journal supplied to the Muslim community and the lead and encouragement it offered to them has during the last fifty years borne by no means discouraging results.

Freedom from Literary Convention.—In the chapters on Literary Revolt and New Forms and Technique, we have already discussed at some length the bold attempt made by Ḥālī, Shiblī and Āzād to break through literary con-

[1] Special translation.

vention in the matter of diction and technique and allow their poetic utterance a freedom such as Urdu poetry had never enjoyed before. We shall here merely point out that the same freedom was exercised in the choice of subjects and in the aim of poetic presentation. The conventional theme of love and wine and cup-bearer with all its esoteric ramifications, or of fulsome flattery, which seemed to cover the whole field over which Urdu poetry for long had wandered in borrowed plumage, in bland ignorance of its true function in literature, was swept aside. In its place life as it actually was, with all its perplexities, doubts, disappointments, sorrows, joys and pleasures, lived in the midst of an illimitable creation of nature with which it seemed to possess mysterious connections, came to form an unending topic for poetic treatment.

"Some word of the people's ills from us you will hear;
Some word of our fall in men's esteem you will hear;
Romances of Qays and Kūhkan *we* have forgotten;
If you want one—*our own tale* you will hear."[1]

In his address to his Muse, Ḥālī gives us indications of what, under the influence of English literary ideals, he came to regard as the qualities, aims, and functions of true poetry in contrast to the conventional, artificial and insincere poetic utterances of the preceding generation of Urdu poets:

"My Muse! if thou be not heart-entrancing, it is no sorrow;
But, pity on thee! if thou be not heart-melting, Thou!
Though the whole world be spell-bound in allegiance to artifice,
Courage! From thy own *simplicity* turn not back, Thou!
If the precious gem of *sincerity* is in thy own nature,
Independent of applause from the present age art Thou!

If thou canst not make the world turn to look on thy *beauty*,
Look at thyself! Take a pride in thy own being, Thou!
The deep sea of reality thou hast made heaving with waves;
Thou shalt sink the ship of imposture, and yet, survive, Thou!
Those days are gone, when *lies* were the creed of verse-making;
Now, should the Qibla shift that way, do not worship thither,
Thou!

[1] *Quatrains of Ḥālī*, by G. E. Ward.

If to live within the eyes of men of insight is precious,
With those bereft of *vision* hold no compromises, Thou !
Should men sniff at thy new-fangled medicine,
Hold them excused :—if so be, thou art a wise physician, Thou !
In stillness, with thy truth, build up a *home in people's hearts* ;
Lift not on high the banner of refinement yet, Thou !
Mistaken for a thief, point out the *road to the benighted* ;
If thou wishest for the long life of Khiẓr, Thou !

Honour's secret lies hidden in the *service of one's country* ;
Think thyself to be Maḥmud, if thou art Ayāz, Thou !
O Muse ! since thou hast cast thyself upon the straight path,
Begin not now to look upon its ups and downs, Thou !
If a new world is to be conquered, do thou go forth, and take—
Clear of the hugging rafts—thy own ship, Thou !
Value for truth shall come ;—but after great travail ;
If there be an instance to the contrary, think it rare, Thou !
Should any recognise thy merit, count him as one gained ;
Ḥālī has pride in thee :—have a pride in him, Thou ! "[1]

(ii) Spirit of Inquiry and Search for Truth

The spirit of rational inquiry and of search for truth which is at the basis of the intellectual equipment, extended knowledge and material progress of modern Europe, has also, like the spirit of freedom, affected Indian thought and found expression not only in the publication of works, mostly of the nature of text-books, dealing with different sciences about man and the universe, such as astronomy, geography, geology, zoology, botany, physics, chemistry, medicine and surgery, psychology and spiritual phenomena, sociology, ethics, economics, politics and jurisprudence, but also in literature.

It is not necessary to discuss the works on sciences here for the reason that they do not come under literature proper, and also because they explain themselves.

We shall therefore proceed to trace the spirit under reference in the several departments of literature where fidelity to truth and nature, which is a distinctive feature of the spirit of inquiry, is expected to predominate. We may classify them broadly under the following heads : Treatment

[1] *Quatrains of Ḥālī*, by G. E. Ward. One or two slight verbal changes have been introduced into this translation.

of History; of Religion and Sociology; and of Man and Nature, in purely creative literature.

Treatment of History.—We have included History for consideration here not merely because it is on the border-line between pure science and pure literature and possesses a greater literary value than works on pure sciences, but chiefly because it forms the background to a considerable section of Urdu literature produced during recent years. What the historians like Shiblī, Ẓakāu'llah have unearthed and resuscitated or vitalised from the past of Islam, novelists like Sharar have visualised through their imagination and idealised in such works as *Ḥasan Angilina*, *Manṣūr Mohanā* and *'Azīz Virgina*, writers of miscellaneous literature like Sir Sayyid Aḥmad and Naẕīr Aḥmad, and poets like Ḥālī have freely utilised as an aid to the presentation of their themes, and Iqbāl has fallen back upon for his emotional idealism.

Hence it is that the historical literature in Urdu is of material importance to the discussion of our subject. We are interested to know whether the picture of the Islamic past as drawn by the historians which has inspired and been so freely used in Urdu literature is a faithful and complete picture. In other words, have the historians in their reconstruction of the past been loyal to historical truth?

Of the several historians who have worked in this direction, the name of Shiblī stands foremost. Through his *Royal Heroes of Islam*, *Sīratᵘ'n-Nu'mān*, *al-Fārūq*, *al-Ghazālī*, *al-Ma'mūn*, *al-Hārūn*, *Sawāniḥ-i-'Umri-Mawlānā-i-Rūm*, *Awrangzayb*, *Sīratᵘ'n-Nabi*, *Rasā, il-i-Shiblī*, and other minor writings, he has done more than any other Indian Muslim writer to vivify the past for the benefit of the present generation.

It may be recalled that in his *Royal Heroes of Islam* he laid down certain aims which would guide him in his researches—aims such as would enable him to ascertain the truth, the whole truth and nothing but the truth, and thereby to present the past as it actually was. This meant, according to him, not only the investigation of historical facts and events, but, what is no less important, the study of the civilisation of the age and of the complex ideas and movements permeating it.

The aims as such are obviously the right aims. But the question for consideration is how far Shiblī has adhered to them in the actual execution of his work. Has he drawn a comprehensive and faithful picture? Has he been true to facts and shown the dark as well as the bright side?

Judging from his writing, it must be admitted that Shiblī seems to have fallen away from his standards. In his eagerness to emphasise those aspects of Islamic history often misrepresented or overlooked by Western writers, he has sometimes failed to dwell on the seamy side as well, and so to make the picture complete and faithful. Not only this, but in his selection and presentation of subjects he has confined himself to the study of great historical personages—Caliph 'Umar, Harūnu'r-Rashīd, Mamūn, and Awrangzayb, and has seldom attempted to get behind them to the leading ideas of the time—religious, social, and political—of which they were more or less the embodiment.

These shortcomings are even more pronounced in the case of the other writers mentioned above, whether novelists, poets, or essayists, who were not avowedly historians. Hence it is that the spirit of impartial inquiry and of fidelity to truth has not, so far, been allowed to work itself out fully in the treatment of history in the Urdu language.

Treatment of Religion and Sociology.—The spirit of rationalism and inquiry has invaded even the field of religious and social literature. We bring it under our discussion for the very same reason as we did the literature dealing with History, for the knowledge of the religion of Islam which this spirit has made manifest has, like the new knowledge of Islamic history, formed an essential background to a great many writings, including some of the best poems of Ḥālī and Iqbāl.

Two names stand out prominently in this connection as having contributed materially to the promotion of knowledge in religious and social subjects—Sir Sayyid Aḥmad and Mīrzā Ghulām Aḥmad Qādiyānī. As we have already referred to their principal writings elsewhere, as an expression of their determination to free their minds from the authority and hold of tradition and find out the truth for themselves, we shall not have much to say about them in this place. We shall merely indicate here the spirit in which they proceeded to ascertain the truth, and the amount of success which attended their efforts.

To us the latter aspect is of greater importance than the former. For the desire for freedom from intellectual subjection and to judge things for themselves is a very commendable attitude, but it is liable to lead into dangers unless the inquiry is pursued on sound and rational lines and solely in the interests of knowledge and of truth.

When we look into the works of the two writers, we find a close similarity in their methods to clear the religion of Islam, as embodied in the Qur'ān and exemplified in the life of the Prophet, of all the later accretions and overgrowth which had obscured and disfigured it. But in the presentation of their results and the application of their knowledge they differ fundamentally from each other. Sir Sayyid Aḥmad's interest in his researches is that of a scholar. He keeps himself entirely in the background. He elucidates the truth, and lets the truth speak out for itself, and be a guidance for his community. Mīrzā Ghulām Aḥmad Qādiyānī, on the other hand, uses his scholarship for personal ends. Instead of presenting the religion as it was originally designed, he reads into it strange ideas and meanings and creates a creed of his own in support of his contention that he was the Promised Messiah and that Islam should be interpreted and followed through him.

It is not, evidently, necessary to dilate on an aspect like this. We have merely drawn attention to it to show that the spirit of inquiry and regard for truth has had in the field of religious and social literature its own limitations.

Treatment of Man.—We shall now take literature pure and simple, the literature of self-expression, of description, and delineation, as chiefly represented in lyrical poetry, in drama and novel. As the field of survey is so vast, we can at best suggest only in very broad outline how far this literature is an expression of truth; how far the writers are true to themselves in their self-expression, how far their descriptions of human nature correspond to reality, and how far their creations are true to life, grow and develop along natural lines in the action and reaction of character and circumstance.

Self-Expression.—We have already seen how the prosodic system borrowed from Persian had narrowed down the scope and nature of poetic utterance. With the rise of the new school of poets, and the reaction against convention which it implied, poetry undoubtedly has become more sincere. No longer is the feeling borrowed from the Persian poets, and no longer is it clothed in Persian imagery and diction. Sincerity and fidelity to one's own feeling has come to take the place of convention and artifice. Ḥālī writes his *Flow and Ebb of Islam* and gives expression to his own deep pain and anguish at the fallen condition of his people. In his *Ḥubb-i-Waṭan* he looks at Europe and feels by contrast what a great country India would have been, had her sons loved her as the people of Europe loved their own. It is a feeling of real love, of humiliation and of a wistful longing for better days. *Complaint of India* is one long spirited denunciation of the share India has had in the disintegration of Islamic life and ideals. *The Widow's Plaint* voices his deep sympathy for the condition of women in India. In this and other poems the poet gives utterance to his own deep and sincere feelings. The same is the case with Āzād,

Shiblī and Iqbāl. The *Khwāb-i-Amn* of Āzād, the *Ṣubḥ Umayd*, and the *Hangāma-i-Balqān* of Shiblī, and the *Shikwa* and the *Jawāb-i-Shikwa* and *Khiẓr-i-Rāh* of Iqbāl, to mention only the more important, are expressions of their own deep feelings and convictions.

Description and Delineation of Character.—The quality of realism in the description and delineation of human nature is, like genuineness of self-expression, a quality which, as we have seen, was absent from the early literature in Urdu. The *Fasāna-i-Āzād* of Ratan Nāth Sarshār was probably the first attempt at the portrayal of life as it really was—an attempt in which others have joined subsequently, prominent among whom should be mentioned 'Abdu'l-Ḥalīm Sharar, Ḥāfiz Naẕīr Aḥmad, Mīrzā Muḥammad Hādī Ruswā, Premchand, Sajjād Ḥaydar, and Rāshidu'l-Khayrī among novelists, and Āghā Muḥammad Shāh Ḥashr among dramatists.

It may at once be stated that these writers are realistic only in a relative sense. None of them, without exception, reveals a deep and discriminating study of human nature. Their observations are necessarily limited by their inadequate knowledge and perception.

Take, to begin with, the social or historical settings to their themes. Only to a certain extent have a few among them, like Ratan Nāth Sarshār, Naẕīr Aḥmad, and Mīrzā Muḥammad Hādī Ruswā, succeeded in depicting the society in which their characters have moved and lived. Others either have no background at all or have something quite unreal and distorted. Sharar, the leading novelist, is a great sinner in this respect. The romantic and highly coloured historical account of Islamic society in which his chief heroes and heroines, 'Azīz, Manṣūr, Ḥasan, Virginia, Mohana, and Angilina, have played their part, seldom if ever existed.

Secondly, the characters in most novels and dramas are static. There is no development as the action proceeds.

Circumstances and situations vary but the characters remain very much the same to the last. Only in the *Umrāu Jan Adā*, *Z̲āt-i-Sharīf* and *Sharīf Zāda̲* of Mīrzā Muḥammad Hādī Ruswā and a few of the novels of Premchand does there seem to be some change in them for better or for worse. In the translations or adaptations of the Shakespearian plays which we have noticed elsewhere, one might naturally expect an easy reproduction of their characters. But so poor is the dramatic instinct in the playwrights that the subtle action and reaction of character and circumstance and the almost unconscious development which at times takes place in the characters in the original quite escape their attention. Not only is the dynamic quality thus absent from the characters in the Urdu novel and drama, but a few of them, like *Harischandra* in *Satyawadi Harischandrā* of Totārām of Meerut, are mere embodiments of certain specific virtues or vices. Besides, in the works of a few novelists, particularly Sharar and his imitators, one hero often resembles another without any distinct individuality of his own. Ḥasan, Manṣūr and 'Azīz are practically all alike, possessing the same outstanding qualities though with different names and moving in different company. Apart from this, there is an utter absence of humour in Sharar's characters, as also in those of Rāshidᵘ'l-K̲h̲ayrī. The language of their dialogue from the highest to the lowest is pitched in the same key, and is too highly polished to represent the real in life.

Similar shortcomings are noticeable in the handling of incidents. In the novels of Sharar and Ruswā and in the novelettes of Premchand there is no doubt a conscious attempt to make action and incident move along in a natural progression. But in the rest there is a decided lack of naturalness and continuity. Things happen unexpectedly and in a way different from what the situation demands.

Such are some of the defects and limitations of Urdu writers which go to prove that the spirit of realism and fidelity to nature has not yet found true and adequate expression in their works.

Treatment of Nature.—The treatment of nature is by no means an entirely new feature in Urdu literature. The early Urdu poets often followed the example of the Persians and employed their knowledge of nature in their compositions. But this knowledge was, however, so limited, and their power of observation so undeveloped, and their interest in it so conventional, that they hardly let it influence their thought and feeling to an appreciable extent.

They indeed sang of nature, but their choice of natural objects and phenomena did not extend beyond a few flowers, rose, hyacinth, narcissus and violet; one or two trees noted for their beauty of form, the cypress and the box tree; one or two rivers, the Oxus and the Euphrates; a few birds, the nightingale, the turtle-dove, the peacock and the phœnix; a few planets, the Sun, Moon, Mars and Jupiter; and the spring and the zephyr.

They employed these either in allusion to the beloved's outward features or inward qualities, or to denote the changes of fortune as governed by the benevolent or sinister attitude of stars and planets, or read some obscure pantheistic meaning into them, or, as in the case of the zephyr or the morning breeze, to use it as a means of communication with the beloved.

With the rise of the new school of poets beginning with Ḥālī, this attitude towards nature has to a certain extent been modified. There are signs of an extended interest in it. Nature as nature is slowly making its appeal in Urdu literature. Ḥālī's *Bārkha-rut*, or "Rainy Season," and Āzād's *Sunset*, which set the fashion, have been followed in more recent years by the odes to the *Himalayas*, the *Cloud*, the *Firefly* and *Golconda* of Dr. Iqbāl, the *Visit to the Flower Garden* of Muḥammad Shāh Dīn, the *Thorn* of Sayyid 'Alamdār Ḥusayn, the *River* of Sayyid Ẓahīr Ḥusayn, and the *Bird and the*

Fowler, the *Nightingale and I*, the *Morning Breeze*, the *Flower that outlived Autumn*, and the *Wilderness* of Akbar Ḥusayn Akbar. In addition to these poems expressly dealing with nature, they have in their own writings made many a passing reference to one form or other of the phenomena of nature.

The interest in nature which the new school of poetry in Urdu has suggested, it may be observed, is not the direct result of any accurate observation and deep contemplation of nature, in all its varying moods. There is hardly any indication of it in any of the writers we have mentioned. Much of their knowledge appears to be bookish and traditional. The planetary system still comes in for its good or evil influences on the destiny of individuals or communities. The traditional metaphorical suggestions still continue to occupy the minds of the poets. There is indication neither of that simple love of nature for its own sake, the childlike delight that one sometimes feels but cannot analyse, nor of that sensuous love of natural and suggestive beauty which in an early stage of development seized Wordsworth's mind—a stage in which the sounding cataract, the tall rock, the mountain and the deep and gloomy wood, their colours and their forms were to him

> " An appetite—a feeling and a love
> That had no need of a remoter charm
> By thought supplied, nor any interest
> Unborrowed from the eye."

Nor, again, is the spiritual and emotional response to nature of these writers reducible to any comprehensive definition like the characteristic and individual attitude of Wordsworth, or Shelley, or Byron, or of Matthew Arnold. In fact nature is not so bound up with the thought and feeling and life of any of them. The limitations of their surroundings and age and their traditional attitude are largely responsible for not letting nature and natural scenes and objects sink deep into their life and imagination.

Whatever may have been done so far is mainly due to the example of English poetry which the writers have had to study at one stage or other of their lives, an example which has obviously suggested to them that nature is a theme hardly to be missed in poetic treatment and interpretation. That accounts for the several attempts that have so far been made. The description of nature is becoming more realistic, although it is still far from being faithful and vivid. Secondly, nature is coming to form the background for human emotion, as Iqbāl's *Kiẓr-i-Rāh* and *Golconda* and a few others indicate, although the background is of no higher artistic value than the landscape in the Gray's *Elegy* and the *Deserted Village.* Thirdly, the traditional use of nature for comparison and contrast is but slowly being extended from love subjects to other aspects of human life.

These limitations are incidental to the stage of imitation. It should nevertheless be acknowledged that the attempts of the Urdu poets have introduced, however imperfectly, an element of realism in creative literature which was for long lacking in the Urdu language.

(iii) Spirit of Progress

Another outstanding feature of Urdu literature of the period under review even more striking than the spirit of freedom or of inquiry is what may be termed the spirit of Progress, a spirit which is so characteristic of modern Western civilisation, and which is manifested not only in the greater energy, initiative and enterprise of individuals, and the desire to utilise their knowledge and opportunities for the fullest development of their personality, but also in their ever-growing keenness and capacity for organisation and co-operation for collective ends.

In the natural course of events, India came under the influence of this progressive spirit, through the different channels we have already indicated.

This spirit, when it first appeared, was in striking contrast to the general attitude towards life prevalent at the time both among Hindus and Muslims. While the one community, under the influence of the ascetic ideal and the doctrine of Karma and Transmigration, was either indifferent or passively reconciled to the existing order of things, the other, disillusioned by the loss of wordly power and misled by the facile interpretation of an undiscerning priesthood, lapsed into a mood of fatalism which viewed everything as preordained and unalterable.

It was this fatalistic spirit which was the besetting sin of all Muslims that the Aligarh movement we have already referred to set itself to dispel and counteract. While educating Muslims to the true spirit of Islam, which was definitely opposed to fatalism and which inculcated the duty and obligation of every Muslim to work for himself and for others, the movement exhorted them to march with the times and follow the methods of Western nations, which indeed were the ways of their forbears of old.

This attitude is powerfully reflected in modern Urdu literature, in the writings particularly of Sir Sayyid Aḥmad K͟hān, the poet Ḥālī, Ḥāfiẓ Naẕīr Aḥmad K͟hān, Muḥsinu'l-Mulk, Shiblī, Zakāu'llah, and 'Abdu'l-Ḥalīm Sharar.

Ḥālī is the bard of this movement. More than any other he has through his powerful poems excited the imagination of his people and created in them a renewed interest in life. So great was their apathy and indifference to progress that even Ḥālī with all his optimism at times lapsed into a feeling of despondency.

"Would anyone see humiliation transgressing her limits?
Let him look at Islam, not lifting her head after falling.
That high tide follows low tide, he would never admit,
Should he watch the ebbing wave of this ocean of ours." [1]

"In the desert when I came upon a bare bleak plain,
On which in the rains there was no sign of verdure,
Which the peasants had long ceased to have the heart to till,
I thought on the trophies of reverse of my race." [2]

---

[1] See *Quatrains of Ḥālī*, by G. E. Ward, Oxford, 1904.

[2] *Ibid.*

Ḥālī always painfully dwelt on the past by way of contrast and as an inspiration and stimulus for progress in the present. His *Flow and Ebb of Islām* is one long and sustained cry of agony. In despair of ever rousing his community, he appeals to the Prophet to pray to God for their redemption.

" O sweet and gentlest of Prophets ! Now is the time for prayer.
Strange are the times on which have thy people fallen.
Thy Faith which once with such dignity left her Home
In foreign lands is forlorn, the poorest of the poor.
The Faith whose guests were once Cæsars and Chosroes,
Herself is a guest now of the Poorhouse.
The Faith which once illumined the world's assemblage
Has not one candle to light her own assembly.
The Faith that came to settle the disputes of others
Is now a house divided against itself.
The Faith which the hearts of strangers did unite
Therein brother to brother is opposed.
Neither wealth there is, nor prestige, nor learning, nor art ;
Only the Faith stands—a tree bereft of leaves and flowers." [1]

The same feeling takes another turn when he recollects that it was in the atmosphere of India that his people lost all their great qualities.

" When Autumn has set in over the garden,
Why speak of the springtime of flower ?
When shadows of adversity hang over the present,
Why harp on the pomp and glory of the past ?
Yea, *these* are things to forget ;
But how can you with the dawn
Forget the scene of the night before ?
The assembly has just dispersed,
The smoke is still rising from the burnt candle ;
The footprints on the sands of India still say
A graceful caravan has passed this way a little while ago.

" Yea, by and by, the wheel of Time
Will obliterate all memories ;
We will forget of what trees were we the fruits ;
Where gathered and where sold ;
But, O Hindūstān ! the World will not forget
The treatment we received at thy hands.
Our story will be an object lesson to others ;
Our story will save them from thy snares.

---

[1] Special translation.

"As the Charmer keeps the snake away,
So will thy rulers entice thee from a distance.
Though the field be cleared of us,
Many a blessing will we leave behind
For others to profit by."[1]

This note of painful recollection is only to bring home to his co-religionists the crying need of the hour, viz. to acquire knowledge and move forward.

"O Knowledge! by thee have whole nations been enriched;
From wherever thou hast vanished, there has come decay;
The treasures of the hidden world have been unlocked for those
Races who have established thee as their stock-in-trade.

"Thou, Knowledge! art the key to the storehouse of Joy;
Thou art a willing fountain of delights and profits;
Rest in respect of both worlds is under thy shade;
Thou art a means of subsistence here, and a guide to the hereafter."

"So rich as the region of the West is through thee,
Like bounty, to the East, from thee, O Knowledge! there is none.
Ah, Knowledge! can it be that, like the moon of Nakhshab,
Thy rays of light are *limited* to that one spot?"[2]

Mixed up with this feeling of humiliation and sadness there always went a note of admonition:

"The fathers—secure in their land and possessions;
The sons—with a dream of contentment in indolence;
The children running riot; the young men doing nothing;
Such families are here only 'as guests of a few days.'"[3]

Says he again:

"For long has Time been crying out, ye Musalmāns!
In my Revolution there is the voice of the Invisible.
My methods change and have ever changed:
Do ye know that, ye ignorant of my moves?
Gone are the days when ye despised the World.
Remember your nation and religion can live only by the World.
Follow, therefore, my lead; leave your obstinacy;
Watch my moves, and turn when I turn away."[4]

---

[1] *Complaint of India.* Special translation.
[2] See *Quatrains of Ḥālī*, by G. E. Ward, Oxford, 1904.
[3] *Ibid.*
[4] See *Majmū'a-i-Ḥālī*, Delhi, 1890. Special translation.

That was the gospel of the Aligarh movement which Ḥālī voiced through his different poems, a gospel which bade the Indian Muslim in the words of the Prophet to march with the times," and not to "abuse Time, for God is Time," and imbibe from the West "all that was *pure*," noble and of good report, for the leaders of the movement felt strongly convinced that in that lay the salvation of their community.

During recent years there has come about a certain reaction against this ideal, particularly in that section of the community which has been influenced by the rise of pan-Islamism. Of this reaction the chief exponent is the poet Dr. Iqbāl. In his *Jawāb-i-Shikwa* and *Khiẓr-i-Rāh* he gives expression to his suspicion and distrust of the spread of modern European culture and civilisation among the Mussulmans.

> "This new wine will weaken the mind still further;
> This new light will only intensify the darkness." [1]

He has no faith in modern democracy and in democratic institutions. They will not promote the happiness of Muslims, nor contribute to their progress.

> "The democracy of the West is the same old organ,
> Which strikes the selfsame note of Imperialism;
> That which thou regard'st as the fairy Queen of Freedom,
> In reality is the demon of autocracy clothed in the garb of deception.
> Legislation, reforms, concessions, rights and privileges
> In the materia medica of the West are but sweet narcotics.
> The heated discussions of assemblies
> Are the camouflage of capitalists.
> Thou takest mere illusion for a garden,
> O thou fool! a cage for the nest." [2]

Iqbāl's ideal is a return to the past, to the life and ways of the Prophet. How that will conflict with the progressive

[1] See *Jawāb-i-Shikwa.* Special translation.
[2] See *Khiẓr-i-Rāh.* Special translation.

spirit of modern civilisation, he nowhere explains. As we have seen, Ḥālī too invites his community to return to the past and follow the spirit of the Prophet's life and work, which, he clearly points out in his *Musaddas* and other poems, is, far from being antagonistic, essentially in agreement with the salient features of European civilisation. In the absence, therefore, of any clear indications in the Urdu writings of Iqbāl as to what he means, we may venture to think that he probably wishes to emphasise what Ḥālī takes for granted, viz. that side by side with intellectual and material progress, the place of religion in life ought to be duly recognised, a view in which none of his co-religionists will have any reason to disagree.

Whatever interpretation may be put on Iqbāl's attitude in this respect, we find that there is in the literature of the period taken as a whole a strong and deep undercurrent of the spirit of progress, a spirit which, like rationalism and the spirit of freedom described already, has, in spite of temporary set-backs and limitations, steadily grown stronger with the growing consciousness of the Muslim community as an important and integral element in the national life of India.

CONCLUSION

When we look back upon the rise, growth and development of the Urdu language—how, after centuries of existence merely as a spoken tongue of Delhi and its neighbourhood, it came to receive literary cultivation since the advent of Muslims into Northern India, how it rapidly incorporated words and expressions from Persian and through Persian from Arabic and became highly Persianised, how in the hands of Muslim writers it came to be employed for the production of poetic literature modelled entirely on Persian example, how this literature was at the beginning of the nineteenth century sterile owing to its artificial and conventional character, how the influx of new ideas and ideals from the West infused fresh life into it, and set it again on its way to progress—when we reflect on all this, we feel greatly impressed by the marvellous capacity of the language to withstand and profit by the vicissitudes of time and circumstance.

Interested as we were in its development under British influence, we have seen how the ideals on which its early literature was nursed came into conflict with others of a different character which reached the country through diverse channels—principally through English literature, and how, as a result of this struggle, it has had to abandon some of its old ideals and imbibe and incorporate into it the newer ones, and how this process of assimilation has been impeded partly by the persistence of old tastes and prejudices, partly by the intellectual equipment of the writers themselves, and partly also by the unwillingness of some of them, owing largely to considerations of prestige, to receive with an open mind anything superior belonging to other nations,

Hence it is that while in prose, where there were no early ideals to contend with, new forms of compositions have been freely borrowed from English literature, in verse no fresh form has been permanently incorporated, although some attempts were made to do so. Likewise, in the choice of subjects and the method and spirit of their presentation, there have been limitations, though no doubt a considerable advance has been effected on what was possible under the old ideals.

Nevertheless the net result has been far from discouraging. In fact, considering the character of the early Urdu literature, and the shortness of the period of operation of English literary ideals, and the conditions under which they have had to operate, the achievement has been very striking indeed.

The poetic utterance is no longer hedged in by serious forms of artificial restrictions. Forms such as the *Ghazal* and *Qaṣīda* are seldom attempted now by the leading poets. In their place, *Musaddas*, *Maṣnawi*, *Tarji'-Band*, *Tarkīb-Band*, and *Qita'*, so much neglected in former times, have become popular, affording poetic thought as much freedom of expression as any form in English requiring rhyme arrangement. The new forms in prose, such as "essay," "review," "newspaper article," "novel," "novelette," "short story," "modern drama," "biography," "history," and "literary criticism"—all based on English example—have expanded the scope and usefulness of the language as a vehicle of expression.

In the choice of subjects and the method of treatment the newer ideals have come to stay. No longer do the writers harp incessantly on insincere and conventional love. Life in all its diversity and complexity, and Nature in all its varying forms and moods, are through verse and prose beginning to take their legitimate place in literature. False imagery, sentiment and exaggeration are disappearing, and almost for the first time in the history of Urdu literature regard is being shown to simplicity, naturalness and fidelity to truth.

These are distinct achievements. One has to remember that it is but the beginning of a "Renaissance" in Urdu, rather, a transition to it. As time passes, with the spread of education and the refinement of public taste and the growth of a healthy communal and national life of which literature is the inevitable expression, there is every reason to hope that Urdu literature will become richer, more varied and more original.

INDEX TO AUTHORS AND WORKS

Made and Printed in Great Britain.
Richard Clay & Sons, Limited,
Printers, Bungay, Suffolk.

CPSIA information can be obtained at www.ICGtesting.com
Printed in the USA
BVOW11s0144200715

409395BV00001B/86/P

9 781406 714111